WHAT HAPPENS IN LITERATURE

WHAT
HAPPENS
IN
LITERATURE

A Student's Guide to Poetry
Drama and Fiction

BY

EDWARD W. ROSENHEIM, JR.

THE UNIVERSITY OF
CHICAGO PRESS

PN
45
R6

Library of Congress Catalog Number: 60-15458

The University of Chicago Press, Chicago 37
The University of Toronto Press, Toronto 5, Canada

© 1960 by The University of Chicago. Published 1960
Third Impression 1961
Composed and printed by The University of Chicago Press
Chicago, Illinois, U.S.A.

PREFACE

This book is largely a product of the introductory course in the Humanities in the College of the University of Chicago. As such, it is, in a sense, a companion volume to Joshua C. Taylor's *Learning To Look* and Grosvenor W. Cooper's *Learning To Listen*, two books which introduce the reader, in ways characteristic of that course, to experiences in the visual and musical arts. And thereon hangs one of the most vexing questions which have faced the author of the present volume, namely that of a title. "Learning To Read," however neatly it parallels the names of the earlier books, is not a title calculated to flatter the prospective user of this volume.

I have often been tempted, nonetheless, to adopt such a title, in the interests of truth, if not of salesmanship. For this book does seek to encourage habits of reading which, as most teachers of college English will attest, have been largely neglected in the education of many of the freshmen we encounter in our classes.

It is not that American adults, young and old, are incapable of several, quite difficult kinds of reading. Their literacy clearly rises to the challenges posed by news analyses, instructions for assembling all kinds of knocked-down equipment, and exhaustive accounts of rocketry, politics, psychiatric inquiry, economics, and sports. But curiously enough in a society which rarely hesitates to acknowledge pleasure alone as a worthy end of human activity, the one kind of reading at which we seem relatively unsuccessful is reading for our own enjoyment. To be sure, the lurid galaxy of paperbacks attests our eagerness to be entertained by scrupulous accounts of physical violence and sexual irregularity as well as our clinical interest in the problems of star-crossed hucksters, pure prostitutes, and noble savages. Even the devotees of such works, however, generally admit that the pleasures which they afford are not the authentic pleasures of literature and that their impact tends to be shallower and shorter lived than that provided by, say, a good major-league ball game.

The pleasure which is properly (that is, not accidentally or irrelevantly) afforded by works of art, literary or otherwise, is the pleasure of affirmative response, the pleasure produced, in some measure, by the activities of one's own understanding and imagination. It is a pleasure which inevitably involves a certain amount of effort and which can be regularly enjoyed only by those with certain habits of mind. The course in the Humanities which I have mentioned is centrally concerned with the encouragement of that effort and the cultivation of such habits. It is as a modest instrument for the cultivation of these habits that this handbook is offered.

A glance at its chapter headings alone might suggest that this book is organized in terms of the major literary *genres*, with a species of coda which pays lip service to literary history. As I hope the text will make clear, our interest throughout is not with literary kinds or literary history as such, but with the habits and information which equip the common reader for the most rewarding possible experience with a diversity of literary works, each to be viewed as a unique encounter. Since the relevant habits and information differ considerably (although, I believe, not fundamentally) with respect to such major literary species as lyric poetry, narrative prose, and drama, the differences are reflected in the organization of this book. And we begin with lyric poems primarily because in works of this kind the peculiar properties and pleasures of literature, when it is regarded as a fine art, can probably be seen to best advantage.

Something should be said about the final chapter. In our course in the Humanities, as I have suggested, the object to which our inquiries are ultimately directed is always the individual work. We are not concerned, that is, with the work of art as a tool or document which can be used in the service of literary history or psychological analysis or the various ends of rhetoric. At the same time, however, we are unwilling to ignore the ways in which historic fact—whether of style or tradition, biography, social history, language, or ideas—can illuminate the individual work of art.

We have been reluctant, however, to introduce questions about the historical context of the works we consider during the beginning stage of our course. There are, we believe, certain grave dangers in exposing students to problems of historical fact at the same moment they are attempting—many for the first time in their lives—to apprehend the work in its immediacy, to grasp the elements of an art and respond to their organization within a particular artistic whole. But as the student's capacity for response to the individual work grows stronger, we have, in the words of Joshua Taylor, former chairman of the course, added "a new dimension of study . . . works of art are considered within a context in various senses historical."

The final chapter of this handbook, accordingly, seeks to suggest that the character of a literary work and the challenges and pleasures it affords are determined, to some extent, by its historical context, by the historical identity of its author. In the examination of two poems, one fairly representative of our own nation and century and the other a familiar product of the English Romantic period, the chapter attempts to show that contrasting qualities in the two works, to some extent, may be accounted for by the period in which each was composed. Ultimately, however, the chapter seeks to remind the reader once again that the elements of literature, as well as the habits of reading which they call into play, remain fundamentally unchanged by time and tradition.

I have called this volume a "handbook," and by this I mean quite expressly that it is intended only as a guide for those who, whether formally students or not, are actually engaged in reading—who are occupied, that is, with particular products of the literary arts. Most of my general assertions, definitions, and suggestions arise from the consideration of particular works. The lyric poems under discussion are reprinted in the text, and the references to longer works are made in the frank expectation that those readers who are unfamiliar with them will be prompted to make their acquaintance. Obviously, this book proceeds upon certain assumptions about the character of imaginative literature. I have tried, within the text itself, to make these assumptions clear—to explain why I have stressed certain questions about literature and ignored certain others. Yet I earnestly hope this book will not be regarded as the exposition of a critical doctrine, let alone of an "aesthetic." The ultimate nature of artistic excellence—and of art itself—are crucial and intriguing problems, but not for the student who is making his first acquaintance with literature.

Since, as I have said, this book is largely the product of a single course and since that course has traditionally been taught by a staff who use a common body of materials in the pursuit of commonly accepted educational goals, the debt conventionally expressed by the academic writer to his colleagues has, in this instance, a special validity. It is no more possible for me to name the specific ways in which, over the past decade, most of my colleagues have educated me in the matters I discuss here than it is to acknowledge, save by a very general formula, the contributions of hundreds of lively, curious, eminently educable students who have filled our classes in the Humanities. In writing, revising, and planning the publication of this book, however, I have been aided in certain explicit ways which it is a joy to acknowledge.

Having, in the first place, gently prodded me into preparing the book, Professor Maurice B. Cramer, now of Pennsylvania State University, advised me in the writing and subsequent class use of its preliminary editions with characteristic wisdom and patience. Professor Joshua C. Taylor has offered most useful substantive suggestions and has given me much help in the publication of preliminary editions. Particularly in writing about dramatic literature, I have been aided by the judgment of Professor Russell B. Thomas. The advice of Professor Albert M. Hayes has been of great value not only in the organization of the text but in the clarification of principles on which it is based. Professor David G. Williams has been unfailingly sympathetic toward this undertaking and has provided me, moreover, with ideas which, among other things, have fundamentally shaped my discussion of the Hart Crane poem in chapter iv. For additional helpful comments upon my text I am particularly indebted to Professors Maurice Cope, Harold Haydon, Grosvenor Cooper, Homer Goldberg, John Cawelti, and Perrin Lowrey. As I have implied, our Humanities course is a repository of ideas on which this book has drawn heavily, but in a way which can never be completely acknowledged. It is clear to me, however, that for many of these ideas—in particular as they concern introductory studies in literature—the course and this book are indebted to Miss Gladys Campbell, for many years course chairman and now Professor Emeritus of Humanities in the College of the University of Chicago.

CONTENTS

1

READING LYRIC POEMS

As children, most of us first associate poetry with rhyme. Our Mother Goose verses, our jingles, even the accidentally discovered rhymes we repeat to our playmates are "poetry" to us, something to be remembered and cherished and set apart from the commonplace uses of language. As we grow older, of course, we discover that people identify poetry by many other qualities than rhyme and we learn as well (although some of us never quite believe it) that much of what is regarded as poetry has no rhyme at all.

This early "definition" of poetry—inadequate and even partially false as it may be—is an extremely significant one. When we become aware of rhyme, we become aware as well of the fact that language has somehow been deliberately arranged for the benefit of those who will listen to it. Here we are not confronted with the casual flow of words by which we are asked questions or given information; instead, language has been manipulated and shaped to construct something permanent. Something has been *made* for our pleasure or our edification, and, in place of a mere act of communication, we have been given a *rhyme*, an arrangement of words which cannot be altered and still affect us in precisely the same way, which stands ready always to be read or recited or listened to in the form which its author gave it. The very use of the word "poetry," despite the fragmentary way in which, as youngsters, we may define the term, implies our ability to distinguish between language as it is used merely to make sense and language arranged into a permanent, created whole.

In its very simplicity, this distinction is one which we perhaps tend to forget as we grow more sophisticated. It might be a profitable one to remember, for the approach of the humanities to literature can become so complicated and controversial that we should be grateful for simple distinctions. "Literature" is an elusive term; we hear it applied to advertising and historical tracts and novels and poems and plays. When does a single document, expressing the ideas or sentiments or knowledge of a single man, become a suitable object for study and appreciation as a humanistic work? When are we justified in calling it art? In calling it a poem? Why cannot all works using language be considered as simple communications and dealt with, as such, by the social scientist? Or, on the contrary, if the humanities deal with the individual products of the human mind, why are not all written or spoken communications the proper objects of humanistic study? These questions, which engage critics and philosophers as well as ordinary lovers of the arts, do not admit of easy, unequivocal answers and, assuredly, a simple introduction to the study of literature is no place in which to pursue them rigorously or to offer dogmatic conclusions. It seems proper, though, to seek for such fairly obvious distinctions as can prove useful in our understanding of literary works and augment the pleasure we receive from them.

Let us begin, then, with a tentative definition, drawn from our early recognition that poetry is a product of deliberate, artful construction in language, designed to stand in permanent form, with the capacity to bring pleasure to those who hear or read it. Even at this stage of the game we may have invited some disagreement, to be sure; for there are those who will insist that poetry is best defined in terms of some moral purpose or some motive or state of spirit on the part of those who write it or even some particular kind of wisdom or beauty, lying somewhere in the universe, which the poet alone can capture and communicate. None of these alternative concepts can be proved "wrong," any more than our own fundamental view can be proved "right." But what our definition should provide are the kinds of questions which can be most profitably asked by the reader whose goal is an experience of maximum satisfaction with individual works of literary art. Such an approach implies a concern for what is sometimes called "appreciation," for the kind of understanding of literary works which leads to an increased capacity for their enjoyment. And if, as all our experience suggests, the various kinds of literature are calculated to produce various kinds of enjoyment, each unique, it seems reasonable to ask at the outset, not what such works as lyric poems have in common with newspaper editorials or speeches or symphonies, but what sets them apart from these other products of the human mind.

If we assert that we are concerned with language employed in the construction of works designed to stand as permanent sources of pleasure, it is clear that we are dealing with more than those works which are conventionally considered poems. Quite properly you may suggest that this beginning definition can include novels, short stories, and plays—and indeed each of these literary kinds will be considered. There are, as a matter of fact, those who would insist that all species of pleasure-producing, imaginative literature are, in the most meaningful sense, "poetry." Essentially for reasons of convenience, we shall follow the conventional practice of referring as "poetry" to the various kinds of metrical writing; at the same time we should be aware of an affinity which links narrative prose and drama with the lyric or epic or narrative verse and which sets all of those forms apart from ordinary letters or speeches or historical accounts.

In beginning with a discussion of so-called lyric poetry, moreover, we are selecting that species of writing in which the distinction we have urged seems most apparent. Many novels and plays can be treated very profitably as social or philosophic documents. It is easy in these and other literary forms to move from the unique, intrinsic character of the work itself to the ideas or facts with which the work concerns itself—to ask questions which, while legitimate and important in themselves, do little to reveal the sources of the peculiar pleasure which the work affords.

The very term "lyric poem," on the other hand, tends to discourage our straying from the work in all its particularity. A "lyric" is, after all, a song, and the pleasure we derive from even the most complex and imposing lyric usually is not very different from our joy in hearing, say, a popular song. From neither do we demand, as a rule, unique insights into life and the world; of neither do we often ask whether the truth is being told or whether our knowledge is being enriched or our characters strengthened. Our pleasure in the work which has been written for us is not necessarily frivolous or fugitive—but it is a pleasure which is felt from the work alone.

In this chapter, our practice will be to consider separately several lyric poems, attempting to discern in each some of the more obvious effects which are achieved, and to allow our terms and other analytic devices to emerge as we trace the sources of such effects within the poems themselves. For the habits of reading poetry and the procedures and vocabulary of poetic analysis are surely most meaningful when they are called into play in the experience we enjoy with poetry itself.

In considering each of the lyrics we have chosen, you are urged to read the poem with care before proceeding to our discussion of it. In particular, you should try reading the poem *aloud*. Since, as we shall soon be pointing out, the qualities of sound and rhythm contribute indispensably to the poetic effect, one important dimension of your pleasure can be supplied only when you *hear* a poem read aloud. You should enjoy your experience with the sound of poetry—the more so if you find occasions to read aloud with other people or take advantage of the many superb readings which are now available on phonograph records. As you listen or read the lines aloud to yourself, however, you should remain alert to the poem as a carefully fabricated amalgam of sound and meaning. To surrender occasionally to the effect of sounds alone is a legitimate and agreeable experience, but fine poems have the power to move and delight us in many ways, the more of which we are aware, the greater will be our satisfaction.

Let us begin, then, with a relatively simple verse by the English poet, A. E. Housman:

When I Was One-and-Twenty[1]

When I was one-and-twenty
  I heard a wise man say,
"Give crowns and pounds and guineas
  But not your heart away;
Give pearls away and rubies
  But keep your fancy free."
But I was one-and-twenty,
  No use to talk to me.

When I was one-and-twenty
  I heard him say again,
"The heart out of the bosom
  Was never given in vain;
'Tis paid with sighs a-plenty
  And sold for endless rue."
And I am two-and-twenty,
  And oh, 'tis true, 'tis true.

[1] From *Complete Poems* by A. E. Housman (New York: Henry Holt & Co., Inc., 1959). By permission of the publishers.

Let us assume that, like most readers over a period of many years, you find this poem agreeable and regard it as the sort of work you might want to memorize and repeat—or at least to read again. What are the sources of your feelings about the poem? We have referred to poems as "constructed" products of the human mind and imagination. Presumably our understanding and ultimate enjoyment of such works can be augmented by a recognition of the elements from which they are created. Thus, the questions we ask, while they arise from—and may ultimately serve to explain—our own feelings in the presence of the poem, are directly intended to help us discover more about what the poet has done.

We can begin with the question which appears most natural to ask about almost any work of literature—the kind of thing, for instance, one almost inevitably inquires from a friend who has come enthusiastically from a play or a movie: "What is it about?"

Because words become language precisely when they *refer* to something, literary works of art (as opposed, for example, to most musical works) are inevitably, in some degree, *about* something. Sometimes, as we shall see in the final chapter of this book, it is difficult to state unequivocally the "subject" of a poem. It may also be argued that nothing save the poem itself can say precisely what the poem says. But the fact that we can provide nothing better than an artless summary for a movie plot or an inexact paraphrase for a lyric poem should not deter us from recognizing and discussing the *substance* of the work. The substance or "meaning" in a lyric poem or popular song may have very little intrinsic importance; it may be trivial or fanciful or commonplace, yet it remains indispensable to the total poetic effect.

The Housman poem you have just read is a case in point. It is possible to say that the work is a sort of tiny narrative, told in the first person. One can even go so far as to speak of a "plot," rather artfully uncovered in the course of the poem. The speaker tells us that, when twenty-one years old, he received a warning from a wise man, a warning which he disregarded. Now that he is twenty-two, he recognizes the truth of the warning.

You will, I hope, be quick to protest that this bald statement does great injustice to the poem, that much more remains to be described before we even begin to understand the source of the appeal which the verses have for us. Perhaps you will say that the summary is totally "unpoetic," and if you do, you will be right. You may want to rush into an account of the verses themselves, the qualities of rhyme and rhythm which make the work poetry in your eyes. But there still remains a good deal to be said about the substance of the work—about the way in which the little "plot" is handled.

It is just possible, for example, that in answer to the question, "What is the poem about?" you will come up with the statement that it is about an unhappy love affair. Or, again, you might assert that the poem is really about a young man's important discovery. Or, somewhat more ambitiously, you might argue that basically the poem concerns the rather terrifying way in which, through learning about love, a young man can grow old between the ages of twenty-one and twenty-two.

Any of these accounts suggests that the poem strikes us with a certain emotional impact. We may be at a loss to describe it precisely or, when we have described it, to secure agreement from other readers. It seems safe to say, however, that the poem is neither highly humorous nor deeply tragic—that one is tempted to experiment with adjectives like "wistful" or "iron-ic" or, to borrow the poet's own term, "rueful." Such accounts can, it seems, receive some support from the text itself. As we have said, the "plot" is simple: advice has been received, re-jected, and finally belatedly respected, but at the cost of con-siderable suffering. Yet this bare account fails to reveal the source of our response because it says nothing about *who* has been advised, who has suffered. The answer is, of course, a very young man who has, by his own account, grown much older, yet is only twenty-two. Our compassion for his "sighs a-plenty" is considerably modified by our knowledge of his age, by our feeling that the "wisdom" he once took too lightly he may now be tending to exaggerate.

We can see, even after so superficial a discussion, that our response to the poem is, in some measure, the product of the little story it tells—of the action or occurrences which are de-scribed as well as of the *character* to whom these things have happened. In such forms as the drama or narrative fiction, these elements of plot and character usually emerge more explicitly and more dominantly than they do in the lyric poem. In many lyric poems, unlike the one we are considering here, it is diffi-cult if not impossible to speak of an actual "plot" or of char-acters whom we can describe even as clearly as we have our "young man." Yet, since lyric poetry, like any form of literary art, must have substance, we should be aware of some sort of *development* analogous to plot, some proposition or descrip-tion or question or exhortation which, one might say, is the reason for the poem's being written and which orders and ac-counts for the things the poet chooses to say. Similarly, be-cause lyric poetry is a product of the human mind, we should be aware of the human attitudes, responses, sentiments, ideas, and judgments which are, in an important sense, "character," even though only implicitly reflected in the "speaker," whose state of mind the poem represents.

In a lyric poem, the order in which the substance is revealed —whether that substance be an action, a character, or a simple proposition of some sort—is crucial. In the Housman poem, the order in which the plot is unfolded and facts about the character are made known is an important source of the poem's effect. The poem begins with a sort of "once upon a time" device; we are invited to hear about an episode in the speaker's youth. In the first stanza we learn of the warning, and we learn that the warning has been disregarded, after the time-honored way of thoughtless young people. It may put the matter too strongly to say that "suspense" has been aroused; perhaps it is safer to say that certain expectations have been awakened, that having told us of this single episode, the poet invites us to consider some sort of aftermath.

In the second stanza, the warning is repeated, this time with an added urgency, for here the "wise man," not content with suggesting how costly it is to give away one's heart, actually outlines some of the emotional consequences of such an action. Then, in the final two lines, we are abruptly and very briefly told that the speaker, having disregarded the warning, has learned of its truth, to his own sorrow. And, again, only here do we learn of the speaker's present age, a piece of information which transforms the poem from a potential tragedy or an old man's reflective tale of a long-ago incident into the cry of a boy whose disappointment in a love affair is poignant because it is so recent, yet probably not permanently tragic because the speaker is still very young.

Thus we can see that the poem is *about* a person and a situation which have a certain intrinsic capacity to interest and move us and that the poet has artfully arranged the *order* in which the full facts about both situation and character are revealed to us. In addition, we must now recognize the poet's *selection* of facts to tell us and, correspondingly, the extent to which he has *omitted* most of the traditional details of an unhappy love affair. There is, we note, no direct use of the word "love," no reference to women, no account of the actual occurrences which led the speaker to conclude that the wise man's warning was true. These omissions are significant; they suggest that in some way we have been invited to supply particulars from our own imagination. How has that invitation been extended? What has the poet done to allow us to feel and respond to so much more than actually appears on the printed page?

The answer to these questions seems to lie in the fact that, although the poet has selected only a few details from the almost infinite number involved in the experience he is describing, he has employed *language* in such a way as to make these details unusually expressive; the relatively few words he has used have been chosen and arranged so as to become singularly eloquent. If we look closely at the poet's language, we can see that the entire experience of falling in love is stated in terms of giving one's heart away. This is a pretty commonplace way of stating the matter, but we must recognize that it is not a literal one. We are dealing here with a *figure of speech*. Physical hearts are certainly not literally taken "out of the bosom" and given to another, but since the emotion of love traditionally is associated with the heart and there is generally some feeling of giving or sacrifice involved in the experience of loving, we have no difficulty recognizing the meaning which this figurative or fanciful phrase is intended to convey.

In selecting this particular way of describing love, the poet has, indeed, stressed precisely the aspect—that of giving or sacrificing—which is central to his poem. It is this relatively familiar figure which he seizes upon and manipulates, to the exclusion of all other aspects of love, in order to achieve the growing sense of urgency in the warning to which we have already referred. In the first stanza, in effect, the speaker is warned that *any* gift, whatever its material value, is a more prudent one to make than is the heart. In the second stanza, the figure is treated with increased complexity. To give away one's heart, it is argued, is not to make a unilateral present; something is inevitably received in return, but what is received is "sighs a-plenty" and "endless rue." Thus the warning has its own development, its own "surprise." What seems in the first stanza to be simple advice that the heart should be kept, even though instead one gives away money or precious stones, may lead us to the premature conclusion that somehow the heart is a uniquely valuable possession. But, as the second stanza makes clear, it is really important to keep the heart, not because it is necessarily of great intrinsic value, but because to give it away is to receive, in return, only suffering.

Thus the entire tale of rejected advice and belated wisdom is actually told in terms of a figure. To put it as baldly as possible, the experience of unhappy love is told by means of a *comparison* with the experience of an unwise gift, a bargain in which the "giver" will inevitably suffer. Note that the comparison is never explicitly stated; we are never told that "falling in love is like making an imprudent and ultimately painful bargain." Yet the comparison is implicit, and we are entirely able to sense the relationship between the literal proposition, the literal experience with which the poem is concerned, and the non-literal but vigorously eloquent way in which the poet has made his statement. These implied comparisons are conventionally referred to as *metaphors*. They are usually distinguished from *explicit* comparisons, which are conventionally called *similes*, and which actually occur rather less frequently in poetry than do metaphors. You can discern the difference between the two by contrasting the implied comparison of Housman's poem with such lines as these two, which begin one of Shakespeare's sonnets:

> Like as the waves make towards the pebbled shore,
> So do our minutes hasten to their end.

Comparison, either implicit or explicit, is only one of the ways in which the poet, departing from the literally descriptive use of language, is able to heighten the impact of what he wishes to say. He can allow limited and particularized objects to represent or exemplify a whole great class of objects or ideas. Thus Housman's "pounds and crowns and guineas" and his "pearls and rubies" clearly stand for all objects of value, any of which should be given away before the heart is. Or the poet can exaggerate in a way which does violence to the literal truth but will achieve an appropriate effect upon the understanding reader. We probably do not believe that the "rue" suffered by Housman's young man will actually be "endless," but the depth and duration of his pain is made clearer by the word the poet chooses. Or again, the poet can exploit our willingness to accept certain objects as *symbols*, our habit of attaching meanings and emotional responses to certain objects whose inherent qualities may be sharply limited. Housman himself employs one of the most familiar of these when he allows the heart, literally only an organ of the body, to stand for man's whole susceptibility to love.

The figurative use of language occurs very frequently, although not inevitably, in lyric poetry. It is not, of itself, necessarily "poetic." When the poet departs from literal language, the clear commonsense language of everyday speech, he does so for reasons not very different from those which all of us have for coloring our ordinary talk with various devices. The Housman poem provides an illustration. The literal observations one can make about the experience of falling in love, whether sadly or happily, seem not only threadbare but inadequate to the depth and complexity of the experience itself. It is natural for us to seek, often artlessly and unimaginatively to be sure, for language which does justice to the impact which love has upon men and women. Certainly we can all think of common, slangy, but figurative ways in which our feelings, following an unfortunate romance, might be described.

What is artful—if you will "poetic"—in the Housman poem is not the fact that a metaphor is employed or that the poet has used, as auxiliary devices, certain terms which exemplify or symbolize or exaggerate. It lies in the originality of the central metaphor, the way in which it is sustained, developed, and made to represent in an adequate way, the entire substance of a wise man's advice about love and a young man's confirming experience of love. The fact that the metaphor is non-literal, that it is fragmentary and selective, makes it obvious that *we* are called upon to provide relationships and associations. It is we who supply the particulars of a love affair, who are able to translate the talk of a "gift" into the story of hasty, imprudent, and ultimately regretted passion. And the metaphor which the poet has selected and to which he adheres throughout the poem is eloquent and successful in precisely the degree to which we understand and are moved by it. This is one reason why the fullest appreciation, the fullest enjoyment of poetry is never an entirely passive affair but is, in some measure, the product of our own alertness.

Finally in our discussion of the poem we come to those qualities which, as we said at the outset, provide the earliest evidence for most of us that language has been selected and arranged to create a work of art. These are the qualities which arise from the physical aspects of language, the fact that, as sound, language involves such elements as pitch, duration, tempo, and rhythm, and that our astonishing vocal apparatus can create almost infinite sounds and arrangements of sound. When, in some way, we sense that from the infinite possibilities presented by language as sound, some selection has been made to present what is orderly and agreeable, we are discovering—in an all-important, albeit often elementary way—that we are in the presence of poetry, of language used as a fine art.

It is highly likely that men made poetry for a very long time before they attempted to describe the making of poetry. Even today, most of us feel that the rules, the nomenclature, the modes of analysis by which we seek to explain the making of verses are generally inadequate, often inaccurate. Something always seems to escape our most carefully devised systems. This is, perhaps, because language is a matter of nuances and shadings, of emphases so subtle, of effects so elusive, that no device for description or notation can do full justice to the task. But, just as we should not allow the dangers of paraphrase to prevent our attempting to discuss the substance of a poem, so we must recognize that the poet's achievement as versifier can be illuminated if not definitively understood by our recognition of certain elements which he has at his disposal and an account of how these elements have been employed.

If we look at the Housman poem, what is the first thing about its appearance which suggests that it *is* a poem rather than a prose paragraph? Let us answer, with convenient dogmatism, that it is the arrangement of Housman's words into *lines*—lines not displayed evenly to suit the printer's notion of regularity or convenience, or assigned one to each sentence or thought, but arranged according to some principle of the poet's. And, although there are many aspects of the poem with which we could begin our consideration of poetry as sound, let us arbitrarily choose these lines as the central object of investigation, asking ourselves as many questions as we profitably can about their relationship to each other and the internal qualities which each possesses.

There are sixteen of these lines, and they have been divided into two groups of eight lines of each. We are reminded of the significance of the term "lyric," if we note that these so-called *stanzas* are actually "verses" which might be repeated to the same melody, that the second half of the poem is, as far as physical length and arrangement are concerned, a repetition of the first half. You can undoubtedly think of many poems in which this sort of arrangement does not prevail, in which, for example, the stanzas are of irregular, varying lengths, or which are not divided into stanzas at all. Here, however, there seems to have been a deliberate attempt to use what most of us will recognize as one of the simplest forms of metrical organization, two units of verse which, in their outward form, appear to be duplicates of each other.

What holds each of these stanzas together and makes of each of them the kind of unit whose autonomy we instinctively feel? One answer is as obvious as it is significant: a pattern of *rhyme* created by the words which complete certain lines. For all its simplicity—the almost sketchy way in which Housman has rhymed only enough lines to hold his verses together— there is a certain subtlety in the pattern of rhyme which should not escape us. We can see this rather clearly if we employ a traditional device for setting down the pattern of rhyme, assigning, in serial fashion, a new letter of the alphabet to each new sound with which a line ends. If we use this procedure, we can chart the first stanza in this fashion: *abcbdeae*. We can see here that the stanza of eight lines is really divisible into two units of four and that, in each of these units, a single rhyme suffices to hold things together. Thus, Housman has supplied rhyme only between the words "say" and "away" and "free" and "me"; the relationship between concluding words in the other lines seems to be a random matter and, indeed, the poet has not scrupled to repeat the actual words "one and twenty" a second time. In the second stanza, if we begin lettering anew, the rhyme pattern can be described as *abcbadad*. Here we notice that, in addition to the minimal rhyming relationship established between "again" and "vain," "rue" and "true," the crucial word "twenty" is employed for a rhyme (with "plenty") for which the first stanza has not prepared us. Expecting a stanza which rhymes only in alternate lines, we meet (in a conclusion whose substance, as we have noted, contains some surprises) an additional surprise in an unexpected rhyme.

Thus the number of lines in a poem and the relationship which, through rhyme, they bear with each other provide an easily discernible skeleton, about which we can discover many additional facts. Another fairly obvious characteristic of the lines is their length. Perhaps the simplest, if not the most revealing, way in which this length can be measured is simply by counting the number of *syllables* in each line. If we do this with the Housman poem, we discover that the lines alternate regularly between those of seven syllables and those of six; again there is a kind of simple regularity here, particularly if we note that the rhymed lines (with the exception of our "surprise" rhyme between "plenty" and "twenty" noted above) are all of six syllables each.

But at this stage, the reader is doubtless impatient, for in speaking of the relationship between lines, in terms of rhyme and of length, we have thus far neglected the most arresting quality of the verse. This is the quality which we call *meter*, the predominantly regular occurrence of a pattern of stress, derived from the accents we customarily place upon certain sounds in the language we use. We are all aware that in speaking English (and it is important to note that what is true of English is not entirely true of certain other languages), we achieve a kind of emphasis upon certain syllables—an emphasis obtained by subtle combinations of increased volume, elevated pitch, and slightly extended duration. We recognize that the word "twenty" can be divided into two syllables, of which, we can say, the first is stressed and the second unstressed, or as it is sometimes called, "slack." It is possible, therefore, to develop a simple system of annotation by which we can describe the stress or lack thereof in most poetic lines, for if we designate stressed syllables with one mark (thus: /), and slack syllables with another mark (thus: ⌣), we can describe the first line of Housman's poem fairly accurately in this fashion:

$$\overset{\smile}{\text{When}} \ \overset{/}{\text{I}} \ \overset{\smile}{\text{was}} \ \overset{/}{\text{one-}} \overset{\smile}{\text{and-}} \overset{/}{\text{twen-}} \overset{\smile}{\text{ty}}$$

And we can proceed to describe this line as one in which seven syllables are arranged so that a stress follows a slack syllable regularly, although a kind of "extra" slack concludes the line. If we go on to look at each of the seven-syllable lines (the third, fifth, and seventh in each stanza), we find that this pattern is generally repeated. If we look, on the other hand, at the second line (which we have noted has only six syllables) and at the fourth, sixth, and eighth line of each stanza, we will find that the same pattern of slack followed by stress again tends to prevail, although in this instance the final, "extra" slack syllable is omitted. Throughout the poem, then, we find a dominant rhythmic pattern, one we might establish by using a drum on which we constantly repeated a light beat followed by a heavy one; or perhaps we could suggest the pattern equally well by constantly repeating a word like *bĕcáuse* or *dĕláy* or *rĕpéat*. We can see now that it is possible to describe the lines in this poem in terms of units, created in this instance by the presence of stressed syllables. These units may be formed by a single, two-syllable word (such as *ăwáy*); they may, as in the greater part of Housman's poem, consist of two one-syllable words, the latter of which is stressed (as in *Whĕn Í wăs óne* . . .), or they may fall in such a way as to require the breaking up of a word so that a new unit begins within the word itself (as in the line *Bŭt kéep yŏur fán - cy frée*). Ordinarily these units, which are called *feet*, involve a stressed syllable in combination of one sort or another with one or more slacks. (Occasionally one of these feet may include two stressed syllables or no stressed syllables whatever, as we shall shortly see, but in these cases, the foot is almost always a "substitute" for or temporary replacement of a prevailing foot which we are able to recognize and describe in terms of the syllable which is stressed.) We apply the term *metrical* to writing whenever the character of the feet is sufficiently uniform that we sense the recurrence of the same pattern more or less regularly and are therefore able to describe its prevailing meter.[2] We have, in fact, developed terms by which we can indicate both the char-

[2] The relationship between *meter* and *rhythm* sometimes leads to confusion and is a matter of considerable speculation and controversy. For our purposes, it seems wisest to assume that rhythm is the more general quality, arising from a universal tendency to emphasize or suppress certain sounds, for a variety of reasons, in almost all forms of communication and the product, as well, of our delight in producing or hearing a fairly regular, ordered repetition of the patterns we can thus create. Metrical language, which is of course rhythmical, can be said to employ rhythm with sufficient order and regularity so as to permit our grouping its syllables into feet and recognizing a pattern of emphasis which marks a sufficient number of these feet to constitute a "normal" or prevailing meter.

acter of the prevailing foot in a given body of verse and the length, in number of feet, of any given line.

The terms by which, according to the disposition of stressed and slack syllables, a given metrical foot can be described are given below. It should be noted that, in applying one of these words to define the meter of a particular verse, we are by no means asserting that every foot within the poem conforms to the pattern described; we are, instead, recognizing that feet of the kind indicated occur with enough regularity to impose a *dominant* or prevailing metrical tendency. The following terms, then, provide a quick way of describing the most common kinds of metrical foot:

The *iamb* is a foot of two syllables, the first slack or unstressed, the second stressed. This is the foot which is dominant in the Housman poem we have been discussing and is exemplified by such words as *because, allow,* and *believe.*

The *trochee* is a foot of two syllables, the first stressed, the second slack. It is, so to speak, the opposite of the iamb and is exemplified by words like *trochee, twenty,* and *honest.*

The *anapest* is a foot of three syllables, the first two slack, the final stressed. It is exemplified by words like *ascertain, introduce,* and *cigarette,* although it actually appears more commonly in combinations of words like *in the spring.*

The *dactyl* is a foot of three syllables, the first stressed, the second and third slack. It can be thought of as the "opposite" of the anapest and is exemplified by words like *holiday, happiness,* and *sanity.*

The *spondee* is a foot of two syllables, both stressed. It rarely serves as the dominant foot in any considerable body of verse, although it may be prominently employed to alternate with or substitute for a prevailing foot of one of the patterns described

19

above. Although few two-syllable words in our tongue involve two equal stresses, the spondee can be approximated by the way most people pronounce such words as book̍cas̍e, hard̍-boiled̍, or ill̍-will̍. More often, in verse, the spondee is composed of two, equally stressed monosyllables in such expressions as hark̍, hark̍.

The *pyrrhus* (or *pyrrhic*) is a foot of two syllables, both slack. It can obviously never serve as a dominant foot—and there are those who assert that it is not really a legitimate metrical foot but that, when two unstressed syllables occur in juxtaposition, they must be assimilated to surrounding, more conventional feet which are accordingly modified. Nonetheless, there are many verses in which occasionally two unstressed syllables substitute for and sustain the prevailing meter and should hence be regarded as a legitimate metrical foot. The syllables in question are often those of such commonplace monosyllables as prepositions and articles and are frequently found in such combinations as ˘in ˘a or ˘to ˘the. It is not unusual to find a pyrrhic and a spondaic foot juxtaposed within a line, since these two "irregular" feet thus tend to offset one another by restoring to the line its ordinary number of stressed syllables.

As we have said, a line of verse can be described both by the *kind* of foot which dominates its meter and the *number* of feet it contains. Lines are named according to length (i.e., number of feet) in the following way:

> *Monometer:* one foot to the line.
> *Dimeter:* two feet to the line.
> *Trimeter:* three feet to the line.
> *Tetrameter:* four feet to the line.
> *Pentameter:* five feet to the line.

Hexameter: six feet to the line.

Heptameter: seven feet to the line.

Our account of the meter in any poem can therefore employ terms which describe both the length of its lines and the nature of the foot which is dominant. A poem in *iambic pentameter* (a very common English meter) is one in which the lines are five feet (ten syllables) long, and in which the prevailing foot involves a slack followed by a stressed syllable. Here are a few examples of lines of verse; before you go on to see how they are described metrically, you might find it useful to attempt to label them yourself.

(1) "Away went Gilpin, neck or nought."
(2) "Away went hat and wig."
(3) "As a friend to the children commend me the yak."
(4) "What is title? What is treasure?"
(5) "This is the forest primeval, the murmuring pines and the hem-
     locks."
(6) "I long to talk with some old lover's ghost."

If you understand the conventional way in which line length and prevailing meter are described, you should be able to identify the foregoing specimens as follows: (1) iambic tetrameter; (2) iambic trimeter; (3) anapestic tetrameter; (4) trochaic tetrameter; (5) dactyllic hexameter; (6) iambic pentameter.

The prosodic description of the character of a poem is obviously useful in revealing the prevailing metrical qualities of a work or the general length and shape of its outline. We must not expect, however, that in most of the verse which really interests us we will find a precise repetition of the same kind of foot from beginning to end, or a complete uniformity of line length, or even, necessarily, a series of perfect rhymes. In poetry, as in music, there is an agreeable tension between uniformity and variety, between repetition and change. It is essential to recognize that, although the various ways in which the poet departs from complete regularity may be described by such terms as "substitute" or "variant" or "shift," these are not mere embellishments or tricks, let alone accidents or infirmities in the structure of the poem. Neither uniformity nor irregularity is in itself an absolute goal to be sought; instead, the poet achieves his mission—his effect upon listener and reader—by creating a suitable amalgam of what is expected, orderly, familiar and what is unexpected, irregular, original. The degree to which we find so-called irregularity is never the same in any two poems; it is determined by the context provided by the individual poem, not only technically but substantively—by the poet's "meaning" and the way in which he wishes us to respond.

"When I Was One-and-Twenty" furnishes an interesting illustration. Among poems designed for adult readers, one can find few more regular than this and many far less so. As we have said, the poem has something of the quality of an un- affected song in two verses, designed to be sung, perhaps, by amateurs, to be easily learned, and to be retained in the mem- ory. One clearly iambic foot follows another with very few variations. We should note, however, that the lines are not quite of uniform length. As we have seen, the first, and sub- sequent odd-numbered lines, have an "extra" slack syllable, while the even-numbered lines are neatly divided into three iambic feet. (These lines, by the way, illustrate the difference between so-called *feminine* endings which fall upon a slack syllable and *masculine* endings in which the final syllable is stressed.) The difference is, nonetheless, a slight one; the iambic beat is essentially preserved; the difference in length is only a fraction of a foot, a single syllable; and the regular alternation between the seven- and six-syllable lines is, in itself, a source of order.

It would be possible to characterize these verses as "sing-song," if by this we meant that they possess some of the singable, retainable qualities we have mentioned. Assuredly, however, they are not puerile or hollow or trivial. The reason why they are not seems to involve the relationship between prosody and language and substance, the three major areas with which our discussion has been concerned. It seems very likely that if a commonplace topic, lacking the subtlety of development we have noted in Housman's poem, were presented in the metrical fashion Housman uses, we would indeed have a vapid and uninteresting set of verses. Or, again, if Housman were content to use unimaginative, threadbare language, his metrical scheme would doubtless merely underscore the poverty of his imagination and feelings. As it is, much of the effect of the poem is derived from the apparent simplicity with which an experience and a discovery are narrated. What complexity the poem possesses is in the artful order of narration and in the reader's willingness to recognize that a bitter experience in love is really an involved and profound affair, despite the brief and somewhat fragmentary way in which the poet tells the story. It would seem appropriate, therefore, that the metrical quality of the poem be unobtrusive, uncomplicated, and of a sort the reader is likely to associate with simple lyrics and songs. The simplicity of meter and of language, indeed the simplicity of the basic metaphor, all may be regarded as contributing to an effect of understatement, of a tale told in a manner stripped of all artifice and reduced to its bare essentials.

There are, as a matter of fact, a few, relatively minor interruptions to the complete regularity of the verses. These are not conspicuous or probably even indispensable to the effect of the poem, but it is worth noting the points at which Housman does choose to depart from uniform meter and the effect he attains thereby. In the third line of the second stanza, for example, the "wise man" speaks with a new urgency and the drastic and painful nature of the "gift" is starkly stated in the phrase, "The heart out of the bosom." Looking at this line, we discover a slight break in the meter. The second foot, composed of the words "out of," may be read as a trochee ($\acute{out}$ $\breve{of}$) or a pyrrhic ($\breve{out}$ $\breve{of}$), but, in either case, the nature of the act is emphasized by this conspicuous departure from the prevailing iambic. More significantly, in the final line, we discover the word "oh" —in itself remarkable as the first and only direct expression of emotion and hence all the more eloquent. By its very nature, the word, without requiring an actual change in meter, interrupts the very regular flow which has marked all the preceding lines; we are really forced to pause for a moment if we wish to do justice to the force of the word. And this pause, itself a departure from complete uniformity, brings an unexpected break into a line which, we have seen, contains the major point, the effective conclusion of the entire poem.

For the most part, we detect variations in meter by employing our habits of normal pronunciation and emphasis in ordinary conversation—the stresses we use in pronouncing individual words, the rises and falls and pauses by which we add force to our meaning in phrases and sentences. While we are willing to succumb to the prevailing meter the poet has chosen to the point of exaggerating a few stresses or, when faced with an alternative, selecting a stress to conform with the meter (by saying, for example, $\acute{wise}$ $\breve{man}$ rather than $\breve{wise}$ $\acute{man}$), neither the sensitive reader nor the sensitive poet is prepared to see the natural rhythms and emphases of speech sacrificed to fit an artificial pattern. On the contrary, these natural qualities of speech are precisely what the poet exploits in various ways in order to secure variety.

Among such devices one is called the *substitute* foot. It is simply the use of a foot of a different metrical character from that which prevails in a given piece of verse. The syllables "out of" in the Housman poem are a case in point, although not a particularly dramatic one. An equally important source of variety is the location of *pauses* at various points in the poem. Here, relying upon the ordinary ways in which we pause to make clear our syntax and our points of emphasis, the poet can achieve either regularity or great diversity by the distribution of pauses. In Housman's poem, for example, it is perfectly natural to pause briefly at the end of every line; moreover, as the punctuation indicates, it is natural to pause for an instant longer at the end of every second or even line. Lines in which the syntax suggests a relatively clear pause at the end are called *end-stopped*. If, unlike Housman in this poem, the poet invites us to continue syntactically from one line to another without pause, the line is called *run-on*. As the Housman poem suggests, the repeated appearance of end-stopped lines conduces to an effect of neatness and regularity whereas, we may infer, a greater feeling of freedom and wide-ranging strength is often achieved by the abundant use of run-on lines.

Pauses are of great importance within individual lines as well as at their endings. An internal pause is called a *caesura;* it is sometimes called for by simple rules of syntax or by punctuation; sometimes it seems required by the emphasis we feel compelled to place on such a word as the "oh" in Housman's last line; sometimes it is no more than the most appropriate place to stop for a split-second's breath. The fact that in, for instance, a regular pentameter line there are nine places at which a pause can occur suggests the possibilities for variation with which the poet is faced. In itself, a caesura tends to interrupt the entirely even beat of a metrical line. By using caesuras irregularly and by shifting the location in which they appear from one line to another, the poet can achieve an extraordinary diversity of effects within a metrical framework that is fundamentally unchanging.

We have seen that the technical construction of a poem can be described in a fairly systematic way by a consideration of its lines, their number, their length, their relationship to each other, their prevailing meter, and the degree and character of the variations from the normal and expected which they display in all these respects. It is often convenient to summarize the general character of a particular poem by classifying it as representative of a particular *kind* or *type*. Questions of line length, meter, and the patterns established by rhyme are most commonly taken into account in the definition of poetic kinds. Descriptions of this sort do not, on the other hand, ordinarily refer to the substance of a given poem, although certain forms are, for various reasons, considered traditionally appropriate for particular kinds of subject. Even poems which do not conform precisely to all the requirements for a traditional kind can be described as approximating—and hence sharing most of the major technical qualities of—such a form.

Housman's poem furnishes an illustration of this approximation. Its units of rhyme are fundamentally four lines long and follow the pattern, *abcb*, an arrangement which characterizes many English folk ballads (and their literary successors) and is one mark of what has come to be called *ballad meter*. In the length of its feet, the Housman poem departs somewhat from conventional ballad meter, in which lines of four feet alternate with those of three, yet this alternation between longer and shorter lines is preserved in the alternation between feminine and masculine endings. To say, then, that Housman has adapted major elements of ballad meter for his purposes is to suggest that he has employed a form with the regularity and relative directness of folk art to convey his equally straight-forward but striking story.

At this point it may be useful to mention other common kinds of verse which can be identified through such technical— or, as they are often called, *prosodic*—descriptions. Here are some of them:

The couplet.—Two rhymed lines, one immediately following the other.

The heroic couplet.—A couplet of iambic pentameter, essentially self-contained in grammar and meaning, and hence with its second line end-stopped. Its name derives from the notion that this meter is appropriate for the serious subjects which characterize epic or "heroic" verse.

Blank verse.—Unrhymed iambic pentameter.

The tercet.—Three rhymed lines, each immediately following the other. The term is employed when an arrangement of this sort constitutes a complete stanza. Occasionally in a poem written in heroic couplets, three lines of iambic pentameter rather than the conventional two will rhyme with each other; this arrangement is called a *triplet.*

Terza-rima.—A series of three-line stanzas, in which the un-rhymed line of the first stanza becomes the rhymed line of the second. The rhyme scheme accordingly is *aba, bcb, cdc,* etc.

The quatrain.—Any stanza of four lines, regardless of line length, meter, or rhyme pattern.

Rime royal.—A stanza of seven iambic pentameter lines, rhymed *ababbcc.*

Ottava-rima.—A stanza of eight iambic pentameter lines, rhymed *abababcc.*

The Spenserian stanza.—A nine-line stanza, of which the first eight lines are iambic pentameter and the ninth is an *alexandrine* (a line of iambic hexameter, generally broken by a caesura, which is widely employed in French poetry). The rhyme scheme is *ababbcbcc*.

The sonnet.—Basically a poem of fourteen lines of iambic pentameter. The poem is difficult to define briefly and unequivocally, first, because it takes several forms; second, because, particularly in recent years, poets have departed from even the basic definition involving length and meter; and finally, because through convention certain relationships between form and substance are usually pointed out in the definition of the sonnet. In traditional English verse, however, it is possible to recognize two major kinds of sonnet and, if we remain alert to the possibility of many slight variations and innovations, we can advance a general, formal description of these kinds, as follows:

The *Italian* (or *Petrarchan*) sonnet.—Divided into two parts, the first called the *octave*, consisting of eight iambic pentameter lines rhyming *abbaabba;* the second called the *sestet*, involving six iambic pentameter lines and any combination of two or three rhymes. Thus the sestet may rhyme *cdcdcd* or *ccdede* or *cdcdee*, or indeed, in any way in which two or three new rhymes beyond those of the octave can be introduced and combined.

The *English* (or *Shakespearean*) sonnet.—Divided into three quatrains, rhymed *abab, cdcd, efef*, followed by a couplet, *gg*. Within the fundamental division into three quatrains and a couplet, certain variations in rhyme scheme have often been employed, one of the most notable being that of Edmund Spenser, whose *Spenserian* sonnet interrelates the quatrains through rhyme by the pattern *abab, bcbc, cdcd, ee*.

These poetic forms—only some of the most common among a great number—can be usefully recognized by the student, first because they serve to classify and broadly describe many poems in terms of general prosodic characteristics; more importantly, because in choosing to adhere to the technical requirements of a given form, the poet clearly limits the possibilities of meter, rhyme, line length and total length available to him; finally, because, as we have seen in Housman's poem, many readers will be able to associate certain traditional qualities with a particular form, such as the ballad, and these associations—together with the character of the form itself—may be exploited by the poet in various ways.

We have thus far attempted to see how, by considering certain major elements, we can illuminate the general character of a poem and arrive at a better understanding of the effect which it has upon us. Our inquiry has led us into three major areas, the first of which has been the *substance* of the individual work. This we have defined, in rather homespun fashion, as what the poet is writing about—the proposition he advances, the question he asks, the story he tells. And we have suggested that, even in lyric poems which are not explicitly narrative, we should find something at least analogous to plot—something which must be told or described by someone—which, as the substance of the poem, can often serve to explain its reason for being and the order of its development.

We have, in the second place, been concerned with the poet's choice of language, not in its mechanical aspects initially, but as the mode by which his "meaning" is represented. We discovered in Housman's poem what is true of much poetic diction, namely that the poet has not provided a complete, literal exposition of his subject, but has expressed, through a figure, the one aspect of it upon which depends his attainment of the effect he seeks.

We have finally been concerned with the area which is generally described as *prosody*, those achievements of the poet which can frequently yield profitably, if never definitively, to analysis in terms of lines, their relationship and length, of prevailing meter and of the variations which attend it.

Before proceeding to apply some of these considerations to two further poems, let us state expressly three propositions which should have been implicit in all that has been said so far. The first is that none of the qualities or characteristics we have had occasion to discuss is, of itself, an end to be sought by the poet or an absolute "beauty" to be searched for by the reader. To isolate a plot, describe a character, or identify a metaphor in a poem, is not to discover what makes it a poem—let alone a good poem. It is to take note of the elements from which the poet has constructed the work which, as we originally defined it, is designed to stand in permanent form with the capacity to bring pleasure to those who hear or read it.

In the second place, it must be clear that none of the three major areas of our discussion exists independently, either in the way in which the poet goes about his work or the way in which we respond to it. If you have ever tried your hand at writing verse, you know that your selection of a particular word is determined concurrently by your desire to say a particular thing, your wish to say it as effectively as possible, and your need to meet at least some modest requirements of prosody—say of rhyme at least. Similarly, the poet's choice of a word—Housman's single exclamation "oh," for example—can be seen as the product of the story he is telling, the mode of language to which he adheres, and the metrical context which, as we have seen, makes particularly appropriate this sound at this place. To illuminate the poet's achievement, it is often convenient to isolate substantive, linguistic, or prosodic questions; but all of our experience and common sense tell us that language is a wonderful amalgam of sound and sense, of what we can physically hear, understand, imagine, feel, and believe.

Yet in the inquiry which leads to greater understanding and hence greater enjoyment of literature, we should recognize that these capacities of language are truly the elements at the disposal of the literary artist—that whatever unique and mystic union he has created among them is indeed an artful creation, constructed in an awareness of what language in its many aspects can be made to do.

Finally, although we have treated each of these three major areas as though it were on a par with the others, we must remember that the nature and importance of the role played by each varies enormously from work to work. To at least some minimal extent, all three are present in every work worthy of consideration from a humanistic standpoint—in every imaginative work, that is, which can be regarded as, in itself, a source of pleasure. It is true, for example, that the novel, the short story, and the majority of dramas are distinguished from what is usually called poetry by the absence of prosodic elements—notably of metrical writing. Yet good prose or dramatic dialogue is marked by an effective use of the sounds and rhythms of language which, if less ordered and susceptible of analysis than the poet's lines, can still contribute vitally to the power of the work. In the lyric, plot, which is as a rule the primary element in narrative prose or drama, is often impossible to find and character emerges at most indirectly; yet the poem is inevitably about something. What is represented may be no more tangible than a state of mind, yet it remains the indispensable substance of the poet's creation. The questions, therefore, which arise from our awareness of the basic elements at the poet's disposal are never totally irrelevant. For these elements, in some measure and proportion, are always present in poetry; they are what makes a poem a poem; they account for what is fundamental and unchanging in our approach to poetry. But in the infinite variety of their uses and emphases lies the infinite variety of poems—and the equal variety of ways in which we can understand and enjoy them.

Here, then, is a poem written by Robert Herrick in the seventeenth century. It should serve to illustrate what has been said about the diversity with which, from poem to poem, we find the poetic elements stressed and ordered.

Delight in Disorder

A sweet disorder in the dress
Kindles in clothes a wantonness:
A lawn about the shoulders thrown
Into a fine distractión,
An erring lace, which here and there
Enthralls the crimson stomacher,
A cuff neglectful, and thereby
Ribbands to flow confusedly,
A winning wave, deserving note,
In the tempestuous petticoat,
A careless shoe-string, in whose tie
I see a wild civility,—
Do more bewitch me than when art
Is too precise in every part.

If, as we did with the Housman poem, we begin by asking what Herrick has "written about," we can readily provide an answer of sorts. The entire poem seems to be devoted to the proposition which is implicit in the title: a certain disorder in women's dress is a source of delight. Here, to be sure, we find nothing which can properly be called a "plot," but rather the expression of a conviction by the poet. It is, however, possible to discern in the poet's treatment of his proposition a development analogous to plot—a principle of order which explains the parts of the work, their relationship, and the unified whole which is their sum. In Herrick's verses, the syntax alone offers—as it so often does—a useful guide to the poem's organization. We are able, on this basis, to divide the poem into two parts which coincide precisely with each of the two independent clauses (they can be regarded as separate sentences) to which the entire work is confined. The first of these, occupying only the initial two lines, sets out broadly and impersonally the rather paradoxical proposition about dress which is the poem's principal paraphrasable assertion. The second part consists of a series of particular examples of disorder, all of which serve as the compound subject of the principal verb, "bewitch." Thus, superficially but not inaccurately, we can say that the poem presents an initial general proposition which is subsequently enforced by a series of particular examples. Even on this level, we will probably want to add that the impersonal character of the initial proposition yields, in the second sentence, to a statement about the effect of disorder on a particular person, the poet or "speaker" whose sentiments the poem is expressing.

Even more than with the Housman poem such a summary seems inadequate. Perhaps it is safe to say that such a statement indicates what we have been calling the *substance* of the poem. But, to use a term we have hitherto employed sparingly, a description of this character fails conspicuously to say much about the poem's *meaning*. Most readers would doubtless insist that to say that the poem states a proposition is to neglect a far more important achievement—an achievement much more adequately described by saying that the poet allows us to *feel* and to *understand* a great deal about the disorder he admires. The particulars which he supplies are far more than examples or illustrations advanced to support his position. Through them we are invited to recognize, believe in, and share the poet's joyous conviction. We can do full justice to the "meaning" of the poem only when we recognize that our reading of it is an experience which involves not merely logical understanding but memory, emotion, and imagination.

To speak of the poem's full meaning, then, we move beyond

what can be paraphrased and into the region of what the poet suggests, implies, and invites us to think and feel. Here, therefore, it may be useful to introduce the distinction between *denotation* and *connotation*—the distinction, that is, between the literal, precise meaning of a word or phrase and the implied or suggested meaning or meanings which it conveys. The denotation of any unit of language can be stated in the kind of definition which a dictionary supplies. Its connotation, on the other hand, may be described, but rarely if ever given a precise definition which will seem equally valid to everyone. For connotation involves our individual capacity to make associations, draw inferences, pursue suggestions, both consciously and unconsciously; and it equally involves the almost inevitable emotions which accompany these activities. Clearly the connotation of a word will vary in some degree with the listener or reader as well as with the context and circumstances in which the word is employed.

But though the connotation of a word is, in a sense, "inexact," it remains a genuine and powerful form of meaning— one of which the poet is vitally aware, which he properly exploits as the occasion requires, and to which the reader can respond fully. And if it is impossible to provide a definitive account of what is connoted by the poet's language, it is still entirely proper and useful to attempt a description of the connotative sources of the poetic effect.

"Delight in Disorder" allows us to see how powerfully connotation can act in determining our response to a poem. We have already said that Herrick's lines can be superficially described in terms of a central proposition, implicit in the title and again in the opening phrase, "a sweet disorder." Now for most of us there is something rather unfamiliar, startling, and indeed paradoxical about the juxtaposition of delight or sweetness with disorder. The combination is, at the least, arresting enough to require explanation or resolution. Sensing what is paradoxical about Herrick's proposition, we expect that he will proceed, if not to resolve the paradox, then to make it in some way acceptable and agreeable. The latter is, in effect, the course taken by the poet; the paradox remains, but it ultimately emerges as a source of pleasure for the reader.

What is revealed about disorder is the fact that it brings to dress a kind of human vitality, appealing primarily because of its sexual attractiveness. This is nowhere explicitly stated, but the regular recurrence of words with similar connotations reveals the kind of association on which the poet invites us to draw. This is apparent even in the first two lines. While we have described them as stating in general and impersonal terms the proposition which is central to the poem, we must also recognize that they employ language which vigorously initiates the connotative effect of the poem—the impression, defying exact paraphrase, of the charm to be found in disorder. The poet tells us that disorder "*kindles* in clothes a wantonness." To kindle is to set afire (and hence to bring heat, light, and movement), and, in a broader but still proper sense, to bring life to its object. It is not, however, simply warmth or light or life which is kindled in clothes by disorder; it is "wantonness." The term, on one literal level of meaning, suggests little more than unruliness or disorder itself, but—as the dictionaries reveal—other meanings of the term have come to include unchecked freedom, license, and indeed licentiousness of an essentially sexual sort. More subtly, there is in most of these meanings the connotation of a certain appeal—a seductiveness which, while not perhaps very laudable or comfortable, is natural enough.

In varying proportions and with varying degrees of directness, the poet enforces—and cumulatively increases—the impression of human vitality and seductive charm in the images which follow the opening lines. The quality of disorder itself is in each aspect of dress which he describes. And yet, in describing each of these aspects, he is able to suggest that it is in some way a source of genuine, if subtle, attraction.

Thus the "distraction" into which the lawn or light cloth is thrown is, in the oldest sense of the word, merely a chaotic, scattered state. But more familiar meanings of the word include both that of madness or frenzy and that of something which diverts or captures the attention. In one sense, "fine distraction" merely echoes the paradox of "sweet disorder"; yet the word "fine" (with all its suggestions of superiority, keenness, delicacy, and even purity) combines with the several connotations of "distraction" to bring to the paradox new dimensions of meaning, new suggestions of what can be appealing about disorder in clothes.

The suggestion that clothes can somehow acquire interesting human characteristics through disorder is carried out as the poem continues. The lace can "err" and "enthrall." Its erring is not only unsystematic wandering; we are bound to attach to the term some notion of moral or intellectual, and hence human, error. To enthrall is literally to capture or enslave, but the connotation of amorous enslavement is a familiar and powerful one. The cuff is "neglectful" (not neglected); the shoestring is "careless." In all these respects, the poet may be said to have employed the device called *personification*, a form of metaphor in which human qualities and powers are tacitly assigned to inanimate objects or abstractions. It is not enough, however, to recognize this rather common procedure; we must see that here the poet employs it for the purpose of endowing clothing with special qualities which, in human beings, have a subtle and even disturbing appeal. The task of establishing this appeal is sometimes carried out by the connotation of the same terms which suggest the animation of clothing (the words "distraction" or "enthrall," for example); at other points it is achieved by the introduction of words like "fine" or "winning," which openly express admiration. Yet even such words of frank praise enrich, through their connotations, the diversity of ways in which the charm of disorder can be felt.

The poet's choice of language provides his work with a shape and order which is different from—although related to—the rather austere syntactical organization by which the substance of the poem can be initially explained. In the earlier section of the poem, the language seems primarily calculated to convey the impression that clothing in disorder possesses an agreeable vitality of its own; this impression is never complicated by the slightest reference to the wearer of the clothing—or, until well beyond the middle of the poem, to any observer of the phenomenon. At the proper point, however, the notion that disorder is something to be observed and felt gradually emerges. We find it first in the parenthetical phrase, "deserving note." The "speaker" of the poem appears in the first person with the line "I see a wild civility." And in the concluding couplet, which contains the principal verb of the long independent clause, we are expressly told of the effect upon the speaker, created by all the particulars which have been listed. It is as though this profession of a personal response has been delayed until, having been initiated into the full nature of this kind of disorder, the reader can sympathize properly with the overt expression of the speaker's reaction. Significantly, as the speaker at last reveals his own reaction, he tells us that he sees a "wild civility." Once again we have the contradictory juxtaposition of the agreeable and the disorderly, but here the disorderly is represented by the adjective, while the noun—the thing seen—is the source of delight. In this phrase the paradox is by no means resolved; it is, if anything, sharper than before, for civility, with its meaning not only of goodness or amiability but of the order and decorum of organized society, is almost impossible to reconcile with wildness. But the connotations of the previous lines have brought us to the point at which we can understand and share the speaker's capacity to find grace and goodness in what appears to be disorderly.

In contrast to the rest of the poem, the final couplet is relatively explicit, almost prosaic. Even the term "bewitch," while singularly apt as a description of the effect which might be expected from the kinds of spectacle which have been enumerated, is used in a relatively conventional sense. Here the poet is making an intellectual assertion. He is introducing, in contrast to the disorder which has hitherto been his only concern, the concept of precision, and, appropriately enough, there is precision in his manner of doing so. Even here, however, connotation plays a part in our understanding of the poem—although a different part from that we have already noted. In this concluding couplet we are confronted not only with a condition, but with a source to which the condition is attributed—namely, "art." If art is the source of excessive precision, what, we ask, is similarly responsible for delightful disorder? Because the two conditions contrast, we may be tempted to attribute them to sources which contrast, to infer that if art creates inordinate neatness, "artlessness" is the origin of what the poet admires. We may, perhaps, go even further and, drawing upon the familiar opposition between art and nature, infer that a fundamental quality of naturalness marks all of the specimens of disorder and accounts for their appeal. But although the *appearance* of these phenomena may be natural rather than artificial, there is considerable reason to feel that this appearance is actually the product of deliberate, artful creation. The poem itself is, after all, a carefully and handsomely created work of art. The syntactical position of the word "art" (as the subject of a subordinate clause which has no parallel elsewhere in the sentence) suggests that to art belong the alternative choices of either being "too precise" or preserving the appearance of natural casualness. We have already asserted that the initial paradox is not resolved, as it really would be in a poem which hymned the joys of nature as opposed to art. "Civility," however wild, implies reason, deliberation, and control. In effect, then, the paradox is preserved, enforced, and given new meaning if we read these final lines as a plea that art be employed to gain effects which appear natural. With the closing couplet, indeed, the poem becomes a celebration of that contradictory but entirely familiar quality, studied carelessness.

If, following our procedure with the Housman poem, we turn finally to the prosodic characteristics of Herrick's lines, we find that they not only seem appropriate to the meaning of the poem but actually exemplify the principle of delightful disorder. In its most general aspects, the poem can be described in conventional prosodic terms. It consists of fourteen tetrameter lines, with a prevailing iambic meter, grouped into couplets of the kind which are called closed—which, that is, are sufficiently separated from each other by syntax and meaning so that a brief, almost uniform pause is natural at the conclusion of each. Within this clear and modest framework, however, there is considerable variation.

Although the dominant meter is firmly established, vigorous and rather irregular movement is achieved by several kinds of variation. At several points, for example, substitute feet are crucially employed. The strategic word "kindles" provides a trochaic foot with which to begin the second line; "ribbands" occupies a similar position in the eighth line; "into" as the first word in line four and "in the" at the beginning of the tenth line are not as markedly trochaic, but likewise depart clearly from the dominant iambic pattern. Again, we find such a word as "tempestuous"—perhaps the strongest statement of disorder in the entire poem—requiring that its extra syllable either be added to the line or hastily slurred over.

Another source of variation in the poem can be found in the shifting location of pauses. Each of the couplets tends to be closed (that is, there is a rather clear pause at the conclusion of each pair of rhymed lines). The first lines of the couplets, however, are by no means uniform in this respect. Thus it is natural to pause briefly between lines one and two; the former contains the subject of the sentence and the latter its predicate. But in most of the other lines there is, to varying degrees, reason in the syntax and meaning for considering the lines of the couplets as run-on, although not, in any case, extreme examples of this feature. And while the use of the caesura within the lines themselves is not extensive, it appears clearly (as the punctuation reveals) at least in the fifth, seventh, ninth, and eleventh line—the pause occurring in two of these lines at the end of the second foot and in the others at the middle of the third foot.

Many modern readers will be tempted to find in the poem another element suggesting the casual—an element which may be regarded as contributing quite legitimately to the twentieth-century response to the work but which it is difficult to attribute with certainty to Herrick's deliberate effort. This is the character of the rhymes. In terms of everyday modern speech, it is clear that the lines in virtually every couplet (except, significantly, the last) are joined by rhymes which are "strained."

In each of these couplets, that is, we can achieve exact rhyme (and, in such cases as the rhyme between "thrown" and "distraction," regular meter) only by an emphasis or pronunciation not employed today in ordinary speech. We must remember, however, that what strike us as marked irregularities in rhyme were probably not nearly so apparent to Herrick's original readers. We are by no means sure of the degree to which any of the rhymes required clear departures from the pronunciation of ordinary seventeenth-century speech. And in any case, through poetic convention, poets of the time—and conspicuously Herrick himself—employed these and other "strained" rhymes sufficiently often so that their appearance may have passed quite unnoticed. The preponderance of such rhymes within a single short poem at least invites speculation about Herrick's intention. For us, their appearance suggests ways in which irregularity, deliberate or otherwise, can genuinely enhance the effect of the work in which it is aptly employed.

In contrast to the calculated irregularity of the first twelve lines, the concluding couplet displays an exact rhyme and (with the possible exception of the third foot in line 13) a faithful adherence to the prevailing pattern of iambic tetrameter. The straightforward language and the concept of precision which we find in the couplet are echoed by the measured orderliness of its verse. We may even interpret the disciplined, rather colorless clarity of these lines as an ironic illustration of the results when "art is too precise." At the least, it seems safe to say that the high-spirited, unconfined appeal to our own sympathetic imaginations has been completed and that the firm, matter-of-fact assertion that these manifestations of disorder "do . . . bewitch" is a suitable conclusion to the verse.

In comparison with the gay, unrestrained buoyancy of "Delight in Disorder," this attempt to suggest the particular sources of its appeal may well appear to be a rather leaden pursuit of a poetic secret which, in the last analysis, defies discovery and definition. Yet the details we have examined should reveal that the effect of the poem and the claims which it is able to make upon our experience, our sentiments, our capacity for association, are the result of careful choice and deliberate construction. To recognize and appreciate the artistic considerations which account for our pleasure in a work can become an easy and agreeable habit—and one which, as is the case with any form of significant human achievement, can ultimately augment the pleasure. Let us, therefore, examine a third, rather longer poem on the assumption that many of the fundamental qualities we have discussed in connection with the two preceding works will be apparent to the reader and, as a result, do not require detailed scrutiny here.

Our poem is "To Autumn," written by John Keats in 1820:

To Autumn

Season of mists and mellow fruitfulness,
　　Close bosom-friend of the maturing sun;
Conspiring with him how to load and bless
　　With fruit the vines that round the thatch-eaves run;
To bend with apples the moss'd cottage trees,
　　And fill all fruit with ripeness to the core;
　　　To swell the gourd, and plump the hazel shells
With a sweet kernel; to set budding more,
　　And still more, later flowers for the bees,
　　Until they think warm days will never cease,
　　　For summer has o'er-brimmed their clammy cells.

Who hath not seen thee oft amid thy store?
　　Sometimes whoever seeks abroad may find
Thee sitting careless on a granary floor,
　　Thy hair soft-lifted by the winnowing wind;
Or on a half-reaped furrow sound asleep,
　　Drows'd with the fume of poppies, while thy hook
　　　Spares the next swath and all its twined flowers;

And sometimes like a gleaner thou dost keep
  Steady thy laden head across a brook;
  Or by a cider-press, with patient look,
    Thou watchest the last oozings, hours by hours.

Where are the songs of spring? Ay, where are they?
  Think not of them, thou hast thy music too,—
While barred clouds bloom the soft-dying day,
  And touch the stubble-plains with rosy hue;
Then in a wailful choir the small gnats mourn
  Among the river sallows, borne aloft
    Or sinking as the light wind lives or dies;
And full-grown lambs loud bleat from hilly bourn;
  Hedge-crickets sing; and now with treble soft
  The redbreast whistles from a garden-croft;
    And gathering swallows twitter in the skies.

If we attempt to provide a preliminary description of the poem by isolating its substance, by the identification of a plot or situation or expository discourse, our results will be somewhat barren—for even the minimal framework we can produce with such a procedure will appear quite trivial and inconclusive. We can say, to be sure, that the entire poem is a monologue, addressed by the speaker to autumn itself. We can further say that the first stanza addresses autumn and (in what is actually an uncompleted sentence, despite the concluding period) describes its powers at some length; we can add that the second stanza poses a rhetorical question, obliquely answered by a series of personifications; and we can finally describe the third stanza as another rhetorical question, reassuringly answered by a series of examples. Such a fragile account can hardly be said to begin a description of the poem, yet we must note, even in this poem, that the monologue addressed to autumn, the rhetorical questions and answers, provide the "occasion" for the rather complex and moving things which are actually said by the poet.

It is, however, in the quality of the poet's language, rather than in the ordered exposition of a plot or argument, that we must find not only the chief sources of the poem's effect but even the principles by which it achieves movement and order. To the question, "What is the poem about?" our answer must be that it is about autumn—not as the season can be systematically described, but as we are induced to imagine its sights and its sounds. And we are able to imagine these sights and sounds not by a story or account or even in a very serious sense a one-sided conversation with autumn; our response is, instead, primarily the result of a series of *images*.

The terms *image* and *imagery,* as they apply to poetry, are the subject of considerable critical discussion. For our purposes, it is probably best to adhere rather closely to the kind of conventional meaning the dictionary will supply. In poetry, then, an image seeks to convey to the mind the *sensory* aspects of an object or experience—to create within us, by appealing to our memories and imaginations, an impression of how things look or feel or sound or smell or taste. Since we have already spoken of poetic *figures*, the metaphor and the simile, it may be well to distinguish clearly between imagery and figurative language. An image may appeal to us directly, literally, and entirely for its own sake—and hence have no figurative implications. Or, on the other hand, it can be employed in the kind of comparison that we find in metaphors and similes. Thus a poet may be concerned only to bring before us the fragrance and beauty of a rose or, by comparing the rose to a loved one, he may employ these same qualities in a figure designed ultimately to celebrate the beauty of his beloved. And, although figures of speech, because they so often are employed to clarify, exemplify, and particularize, tend to involve concrete images, they need not necessarily do so. To say that clothes possess "wantonness" is to speak figuratively but abstractly; wantonness is not a quality that can be understood through our physical senses, except by some concrete exemplification.

The subtle interplay of figure and image is abundantly illustrated in Keats's poem. The entire first stanza can be described as developing a metaphor, in that it is concerned with the role of autumn as "close bosom-friend of the maturing sun." In this role, initially characterized in rather an abstract way, the season is seen in a series of particular activities, and each of these confronts us with an image of great clarity. The majority of these images are plainly visual; we are asked to see, with the "mind's eye," the loaded trees, the ripening fruits, the budding flowers, and the surfeited bees. At the same time, there are points in which the appeal may be to the tactile sense as well; for some readers at least, the imagination can construct the feeling of burgeoning fruit, the swelling and growing plumpness which touch as well as sight is able to discern. It is even possible that our memories of the taste of things are also being evoked. We must note as well that the impressions conveyed expressly by the imagery are augmented by the connotative power of individual words and phrases—the cumulative suggestion of active ripening and fruition conveyed by such words as "mellow," "maturing," "load," "fill," "swell," "plump," and even perhaps (though more subtly) such a term as "bosom-friend."

The second stanza again is sustained by a single metaphor—a personification of autumn, never explicitly described but apparently involving the comparison of the season with some sort of harvest worker in postures and acts appropriate to the time of year. Again, the metaphor is productive of rich imagery, here indeed rather more closely related to the metaphor itself than in the previous stanza. It is autumn personified, rather than her works, whom we are asked to view in various aspects: reposing, sleeping, gleaning, watching patiently through the closing days of the harvest.

The final stanza once more pursues a metaphor which is productive of a variety of images, although here the metaphor is rather less elaborate and, for that matter, less important. It involves, in fact, only the initial, fanciful assumption that autumn is sufficiently "human" to ask for a consoling reminder that she, like spring, has her own kind of music—a reminder documented by the particular images which occupy the entire stanza. And here, while there are visual images to describe the evening colors of late autumn, the movement of the gnats, the gathering of the swallows, we are aware of imagery which appeals strongly to our sense of sound. In enumerating the songs of autumn, the poet is inviting us to reconstruct imaginatively the sounds of insects, animals, and birds, to sense the subdued, agreeable melancholy of the autumn dusk by the quality of its characteristic noises.

Clearly one of the most effective ways in which the poet can convey the quality of sound is by sound itself—by the selection and arrangement of words of which the sounds, as well as the significations, aid the imagination in its recovery of sensory experience. The final stanza of "To Autumn" reveals how the sounds of nature can be echoed in the language by which the poet describes them. Obvious examples are found in such words as "bleat," "whistles," and "twitter"—words which discernibly approximate the sounds to which they refer.

These words whose sounds clearly suggest their meanings are specimens of what is called *onomatopoeia*. This poetic procedure takes its most obvious form in words of the sort we have pointed out; the reader can doubtless think of such other examples as "crash" or "hum" or "whinny." Somewhat more subtly, the physical sounds of words can be employed to produce images which appeal to other senses than that of hearing, to suggest spectacles and actions and states of mind. It does not, for example, seem too farfetched to assert that the word "plump," in the seventh line of Keats's first stanza, enhances by its sound the visual—and even the tactile—effect of Keats's image.

In its simplest, most unequivocal manifestations, onomatopoeia can be seen as one end of a spectrum, a spectrum which can be extended to all of the ways in which poets attempt to follow Pope's dictum that "the sound must seem an Echo to the sense." For in all of the language he chooses, the poet must obviously be concerned that sound be compatible with—and wherever possible augment—the effect he is seeking. The broad considerations which govern the poet's system of meter and rhyme reflect this concern on a general level—perhaps at what might be called the opposite end of the spectrum from the precise, limited quality of a single use of onomatopoeia. Between these two lie the many possibilities for the poet's exploitation of the characteristics of sound, ranging from those treatments of sound which have been found to be agreeable merely because of some such general principle as orderliness or variation to the use of sound in conveying very explicit images or states of mind.

Many of the ways in which the poet manipulates the sounds of words involve *repetition* of some sort. We have already encountered the most familiar form of repetition, namely the *rhyme* which links two or more lines together and is called *end rhyme*. When rhymes of this sort occur between words, one or both of which are within the line, the rhyme is called *internal*. Traditionally both end and internal rhyme involve the features we are accustomed to think of as marking the true rhyme, namely the repetition of identical concluding sounds in

47

words which, in their initial sounds, differ from each other. It is worth observing, however, that the function of linking lines by rhyme can be served by certain other kinds of repetition or, as some of the couplets in "Delight in Disorder" suggest, by approximations of the same sound which are not, strictly speaking, "perfect" rhymes.

Within lines, other kinds of repetition often appear very prominently. The repetition of the initial sounds of words is called *alliteration;* it is a device made familiar not only by poets but by such folk as the makers of advertising or political slogans. "To Autumn" furnishes abundant examples of alliteration, beginning in the very first line with the initial consonant of "mists" and "mellow," which is echoed in the following line by "maturing."

Another form of repetition is called assonance, and this is usually defined as the repetition of vowel sounds within words, such as "out" and "loud" or "wave" and "lake." Here, as in his use of other forms of repetition, the effective poet tends to be restrained and, at the same time, flexible in his use of the device. We rarely find assonance which strikes us with the simplicity and force of end rhyme, and assonant terms are less likely to be directly juxtaposed than to be judiciously distributed through one or several lines in order to achieve a kind of unobtrusive unity. We find this illustrated in these lines:

> And sometimes like a gleaner thou dost keep
> Steady thy laden head across a brook;
> Or by a cider-press, with patient look . . .

The long *i* in "by" and "cider" provides assonance of a rather obvious sort; it is not equally apparent—although perhaps equally important—that they repeat a vowel sound which has appeared three times in the two previous lines: in "sometimes," "like," and "thy." The words "gleaner" and "keep" are linked in similar fashion, and assonance likewise contributes to the quality of repetition achieved by "steady," "head," and "press" in the two following lines. The verses also illustrate the way in which the effect of assonance can be augmented by a repetition not only of vowel sounds but of accompanying consonants. Thus the combination of vowel and consonant which initially links "core" and "more" as end rhymes in the first stanza reappears shortly with the repetition of "more" in the ninth line, "warm" in the tenth line, and "o'er" in the final line; the internal vowel consonant combination of "warm" links it to the other words, themselves held together by rhyme.

The repetition of consonants alone, in internal or final positions of words, is called *consonance.* In the lines already quoted, consonance can be found in the repeated *d* sounds of "steady," "laden," "head," and "cider." Combinations of consonants can be used in the same general way, as in the phrase "soft-lifted" or the recurrent *nd* sound of "friend," "round," and "bend" distributed through the opening five lines of the first stanza.

Repetition, in its various forms, is only one of many ways in which the poet can use the sound of words to gain the effect he seeks. The ease or difficulty with which we can pronounce certain words or combinations of words can affect the *tempo* and evenness of poetic lines in obvious ways. The differences between so-called long and short vowels, between voiced and voiceless consonants, between sounds made in the front of the mouth and those made farther back—all can be exploited to create certain general effects, often difficult to define, yet clearly apparent when lines of different sorts are compared. Compare, for example, the brisk opening of Housman's poem,

> When I was one-and-twenty
> I heard a wise man say . . .

with Keats's single line,

> Thou watchest the last oozings hours by hours.

Although the two lines of Housman contain several more syllables—and two more feet—than Keats's single line, the latter actually takes longer to speak, in any reasonably intelligible way. One obvious reason for the difference lies, of course, in the relative regularity of the Housman verse, the easy, ongoing, unchecked rhythm of its simple iambs. In contrast, the line by Keats is singularly irregular—like a great many within the poem—and, in the absence of a strong metrical pattern to shape our emphases and pronunciation, we give to each word the full weight required by its meaning and ordinary pronunciation.

In addition, Keats's line is simply more difficult to pronounce rapidly. At the end of almost every one of Housman's words, the reader's mouth is in position readily to pronounce the succeeding word; "one-and-twenty" is, despite its hyphens, a phrase that can be easily elided or slurred into a single word. Compare this to the manner in which we are forced to pronounce Keats's single word "watchest" and in which, when we have spoken the word, it is necessary to move the mouth and tongue before pronouncing the simple word "the." Beyond this, Keats, in contrast to Housman, has chosen to use sounds of intrinsically greater length. The vowel sound *ou*, which appears three times in the single line (a splendid specimen of assonance!) is actually a combination of two vowels, a diphthong. And the double *o* in "oozings" provides one of the longest vowel sounds in our language—one that can be protracted in pronunciation long beyond our ordinary treatment of vowels and yet remain proper. Even the consonants can contribute to the slow tempo of the line; the soft (or voiced) *s* in both "oozings" and the repeated "hours" can be sustained longer than the great majority of the consonants in which our words end.

Before we return to consider "To Autumn" in the light of the foregoing discussion, it may be well to point out two matters for caution. In the first place, while the power of sound to achieve effects that are genuine and often clearly demonstrable must always be taken into account, we must be circumspect in assigning to the sound of words *alone*, effects that, more often than not, are also created by the meaning, connotative and denotative, which words inevitably carry. The relationship between sound and sense is delicate and elusive. Whatever gentle somnolence we find in the line we have quoted from Keats disappears if we substitute for the poet's words something which has most of their quality of sound but is sheer nonsense, such as "Thou catchest thy past boozings, showers on showers." In the second place, the mere presence of characteristics that can be described as alliteration, internal rhyme, onomatopoeia, and the rest in no way determines the excellence of a poem. To detect within a poet's lines two sounds which seem to echo each other, to uncover by diligent search certain real or fancied changes in tempo or rhythm is to do little unless such discoveries can be related to the accomplishment of genuine effects upon the reader. Some of these effects, it is true, may be stated in very general terms; it may be assumed, for example, that discernible repetition, judiciously employed, is a rather agreeable phenomenon. But since the poet is ordinarily concerned with providing a particular experience and eliciting a particular kind of pleasurable response, it is natural that he employ the devices at his disposal in the service of specific ends. As we shall shortly suggest, it is insufficient, if partially true, to say merely that in "To Autumn" Keats has used beautiful language. The "beauty" in his language arises from its eminent suitability to his mission, to the creation of a poem which reveals certain aspects of autumn and brings from the reading an understanding and pleasurable response to what has been created.

Returning to the poem by Keats, we recall that a consideration of the poem as mere "statement" yielded results which not only failed to suggest anything save a vague outline of the poem's meaning but did not even succeed in furnishing us with a satisfactory principle of order within the work. Now, however, let us see whether an amalgam of the elements we have been discussing—of language, as figure and image, and as pure sound as well—will not allow us to find the poem more orderly, meaningful, and moving.

Our initial recognition in this process should, I think, be that the poem is concerned with *aspects* of autumn, never expressly referred to as such, but quite plainly described and elaborated in unified fashion in each of the stanzas. In the first stanza we are struck, among other things, by the character of the verbs. To autumn, as "close bosom-friend of the maturing sun," are ascribed various powers, set forth by a series of active verbs: "load," "bless," "bend," "fill," "swell," and "set budding." Autumn, here personified although not in a highly particularized way, is seen as an agent, actively engaged in bringing about the phenomena of ripeness. The very syntax of the lines contributes to this characterization; the parallel infinitive clauses carry on in a series, culminating in a clause of climactic complexity. Indeed the final clause continues as though it itself would "never cease," moving from the ceaseless budding of flowers to embrace the bees as actors in the drama of busy productivity. Combined with this impression of activity is the impression first supplied by the term "maturing"; we have already seen how the sounds and images collectively enforce the sensation of growth and ripeness and rich abundance. And, almost unconsciously, we are aware of a time of year—not the whole of the autumn months, but that early period when the harvest is approaching, when the "warm days" persist and there is little suggestion of winter's approach. We are even reminded of a time of day; the sun and warmth suggest late morning or noon—or at least an hour when night seems as remote as winter. These then are the *works* of autumn, traditional and familiar, but set forth in a series of images which repeatedly bring to us the well-being of mature growth and abundance—and set forth, too, with selectivity, in that many conventional autumn sights and sounds are rejected in the development of a central impression.

Most of us are probably able to sense a contrast between the second stanza and the first, a contrast which perhaps we feel only vaguely at first reading but which becomes plainer when we consider the second stanza in terms similar to those we have employed in discussing the first. To the productive activity of autumn in the first stanza, we can contrast a feeling of repose, achieved by many of the same devices. The verbs here are suggestive; many of them are passive or participial and even the active verbs are words such as "keep" or "watchest." It is possible to say that the first stanza concerns itself with the activities of autumn, the second, with its appearance, but this shift in the aspects of the season which the poet has chosen to present is accompanied by a progression in the time of year. Autumn, as an active agent, has yielded to autumn in the person of the harvest hand (a woman, we infer) in the late stages of the season. The careless sitting, the sleep, the patient watching are parts of the aftermath of the harvest; so too is the steady pace of the gleaner, whose more leisurely activity succeeds the main work of the harvest. In this second stanza, then, activity has been followed by repose, ripeness by harvest, the early fall season by the final stages of the harvest, and the fecund, hot period of full sunshine by the drowsy "hours by hours" of what can only be the afternoon.

In the final stanza, there is little attempt to personify autumn. It is as though at this stage the season had lost its resemblance to any human agent, whether in robust action or in graceful repose. Instead we are confronted by aspects of autumn which can best be understood through sounds. We can continue the seasonal cycle which we have traced through the early autumn and late harvest time and find here only the barren stubble-fields, whose sole suggestion of life comes from the remote glow of the sinking sun. Similarly, we can find in these lines the logical final stage in a progression which has begun in the fruitful, sunlit flush of noon and progressed through the long afternoon hours to terminate at dusk. We can also see that what has begun with vigorous, productive activity and gone on to well-earned repose is now without a suggestion of human vitality, animate nature itself being represented only by the subdued sounds of insects, animals, and birds. And here our entire experience of autumn comes to bear, stimulated by the poet's language, upon the aspects of the season which he has asked us to consider and understand. For autumn is not only the season of final growth and ripeness; it is not only the time for serene, untroubled rest. It is the season, as well, which precedes and yields inevitably to winter, to lifelessness, to the disappearance of all the "mellow fruitfulness" which crowns the processes of life. In words like "soft-dying," "wailful," "mourn," "sinking," and "dies" we find the connotation of death—death not as tragic loss or an abrupt and violent conclusion to life, but as a gentle, inevitable terminal stage which follows life even as winter succeeds autumn. Here is but the implication, the anticipation of death and winter, for these remain the images and sounds of autumn; winter and lifelessness are merely sensed and presaged in the quiet noises of the late autumnal season.

In any immediate sense, the poem is not, of course, "about" human life but about autumn. Yet in his choice of structure, of significative language, of sound, the poet has chosen to present, with great richness, the cyclical aspect of autumn—that aspect which is analogous to and representative of the cycle of life itself. And whether we concentrate upon the day, the year, or the processes of life, we move from abundance and ripeness to satisfied repose and, finally, to a subdued anticipation of lifelessness and night. On a literal level, the poet has merely addressed autumn in terms which agreeably reveal selected aspects of the powers, the sights, and the sounds which characterize the season. On a connotative level, he has seen—and has asked us to share—the spectacle of a season which, in its succeeding phases, reflects the ultimate richness of life and the gentle anticipation of lifelessness—for the day, the year, and all animate nature, including man himself.

Whether the poem gains its ultimate effect by revealing the manner in which the processes of life are reflected in a single season or is simply a richly evocative representation of the cycles of the season itself is a question which the individual reader must decide. Whatever the answer, it seems clear that we can find, in the coherence of imagery and sound within the several stanzas and the reasonable progression from one stanza to the next, the satisfying principle of order which a mere summary of "argument" cannot supply. In the images themselves and in our response to them lies the primary source of development and meaning.

We have been engaged so far in pointing out facts about lyric poems which are, so to speak, demonstrable—qualities and poetic procedures which, one hopes, are discernible to any careful reader. Into many responsible discussions of poetry, however, there are introduced terms which may seem relatively intangible, which refer to qualities of writing which elude precise definition and are open to difference of opinion. One such term, for example, is *mood*—most often used, as in its ordinary sense, to indicate a state of mind and emotion which pervades the poem and is communicated to and shared by the reader. One is inescapably aware of mood in the presence of such a poem as "To Autumn" and, in our desire to speak with rigor, we should not be led to neglect the impalpable but authentic state of spirit which, for many readers, is the most memorable element in the experience offered by the poem.

Another extremely interesting term which is frequently employed in discussions of poetry is *tone*. Most often, it appears, this term is used to describe the fundamental attitude which the poet takes toward his subject, his audience, and indeed toward his entire poetic undertaking. We can probably understand this meaning of the term if we pursue the very real analogy between poetic tone and "tone of voice" in conversation. In reading a given poem aloud, that is, what "feelings" should we attempt to communicate through such properties of voice as volume, pitch, and tempo? Thus, for example, we might strive to read our Housman poem with a slightly wry, "rueful" air of understatement, while the verses by Keats seem to call for a kind of gentle solemnity. Obviously, at any rate, only a very insensitive reader would recite both poems in precisely the same way. And although we might argue about the precise tone that is achieved in each poem (and, consequently, about the "proper" way in which each should be read), our very attempt to capture this quality in a work points to its reality and importance.

There is, accordingly, nothing misleading whatever about the employment of such terms as "tone" and "mood" in discussing poetry. More often than not, they are used in sincere, sensitive efforts to establish what is most basic in the effect of lyric poetry. We have introduced them belatedly because they are best viewed as as describing the *results* of the poetic process. For in any poem, mood and tone are achieved—as are the more general qualities we describe by terms like "beauty" or "expressiveness" or "power"—through a procedure which artfully and systematically exploits the basic facts about language and its capacities. The "tone" of the Housman poem or the "mood" of "To Autumn" may well be their most important accomplishments. It is to understand how these things are achieved and, hopefully, to enhance their impact upon us that the majority of terms and concepts we are considering have been introduced.

In our discussion of three very different kinds of poems we have introduced a variety of these terms and concepts. Some of them can be applied with almost equal usefulness to most lyric poetry. Thus it is profitable to describe, in terms of prevailing patterns of meter and rhyme (or perhaps their absence), the general structure and "appearance" of any poem. Not the least important difference, for example, among the three works we have discussed is of this sort. It is certainly illuminating to note the contrast between the uncomplicated ballad-like structure of Housman's poem and the compact set of seven tetrameter couplets within which Herrick achieves his calculated caprice. And the simplicity, real or feigned, of these two poems in turn contrasts strikingly with the unusual and relatively elaborate prosodic structure of "To Autumn," with its eleven-line stanzas, its repeated deviations from an iambic meter which is often almost submerged, its shifting caesuras, its run-on lines, and its rhythm which arises as much from individual sounds and syntax as from metrical regularity. Similar generalizations about the quality of the poet's language—his reliance on imagery or on metaphor, his syntax, his adherence to or departure from the patterns of everyday speech—again can be very useful in the discussion of almost any poem.

Moreover, none of the major kinds of questions with which we have been concerned is totally irrelevant in the presence of a genuine work of literary art. The unobtrusive simplicity of Housman's meter may not be the chief source of the effect which the poem has upon us; it is, nonetheless, a genuine element used with important, calculated effect. Similarly, although we did not find it particularly revealing to describe Keats's poem as an address to autumn involving two rhetorical questions, this simple device provides a structural principle which is necessary to all the richer order and meaning which the images supply. As we move on to consider narrative prose and drama, we shall find that the novelist and playwright face their peculiar problems and enjoy peculiar advantages because of the kind of literature they choose to write. We, in turn, shall be asking new questions about these works. We shall often find it necessary to neglect certain inquiries—into the quality of sound in a playwright's language, for example—and to pursue very carefully questions concerning such matters as plot and character. But, as we have seen in various specimens of lyric poetry, this remains, for writer and reader, a matter of emphasis and proportion.

What this amounts to saying is that the literary artist—like the painter or musician—is free to make what qualitative and quantitative use he wishes of the elements at his disposal. To the extent he chooses to suppress one element and stress another, the character of his work and of our response to it will be modified. Inevitably, our own approach as thoughtful readers will be shaped by a recognition of the elements which seem to predominate and which lend to the work its order and significance. This requires from us both rigor and flexibility—as well as a species of humility which will reconcile us to answers which are rarely unequivocal and never exhaustive. Yet the indisputable fact about a literary work which pleases us is that it *does* please us. To explore the sources of that pleasure is not only to pursue the natural inclination of a mature, inquiring mind; it is to cultivate habits by which, in the future, similar pleasures will be more frequently, readily, and richly enjoyed.

2

READING NARRATIVE FICTION

The art of fiction is the art of telling stories. It is an art which often strives for effects and employs emphases which seem very different from those of lyric poetry; yet poets, narrative prose writers, and, for that matter, playwrights display much the same kind of thoughtful control of language, which is, after all, their common medium.

Consider the following passage:

Squire Trelawney, Dr. Livesey, and the rest of the gentlemen having asked me to write down the whole particulars about Treasure Island, from the beginning to the end, keeping nothing back but the bearings of the island, and that only because there is still treasure not yet lifted, I take up my pen in the year of grace 17——, and go back to the time when my father kept the "Admiral Benbow" inn, and the brown old seaman, with the sabre cut, first took up his lodging under our roof.

The passage, as you have probably recognized, is the opening sentence of Robert Louis Stevenson's *Treasure Island*. In the construction of this single sentence, the writer has achieved a number of things by methods which are not fundamentally different from many of those employed by the lyric poet. Like the poet he has carried out his task by the skilful selection of particulars and their arrangement in a deliberate order, he has employed words and images with considerable connotative power, and he has even exploited such properties of language as rhythm and tempo. And his accomplishments and the ends he is seeking can be discussed as readily as those of the lyric poet, although here, since this is only the very beginning of a very long story, the passage must be viewed in its proper context.

The sentence conveys, in the first place, a great deal of information—more than we are likely to recognize on a first reading. The tale is of the eighteenth century; the narrator, and presumably the hero, is a boy, now at the time of telling considerably older, yet still deferential toward the squire, the doctor, and "the rest of these gentlemen." He is obviously not a professional writer or, indeed, particularly sophisticated. Ingenuously he begins his book by explaining why it is that he "takes up his pen" and precisely what his instructions are. In his long complex sentence, with its dependent clauses covering such a diversity of points, there is an additional appearance of artlessness. Our "author" is this boy who, with every appearance of honesty, is setting down the "whole particulars" of what promises to be an absorbing tale. The air of earnest simplicity with which, without formal introduction, he seems to assume we will know the identity of the squire and the others is augmented by a clearly "unliterary," almost tiresomely rhythmic piling up of clause upon clause and by the commonplace quality of particular words. Yet unobtrusively, through the references to the island, the treasure, and above all the romantic figure of the "brown old seaman with the sabre cut," we are supplied with exciting suggestions of secrecy, adventure, and even violence.

These connotations alone create expectations, and the suspense they engender is increased by the deliberately unanswered questions which the passage raises. Like an able poet, Stevenson has created a literary entity which, though it must inevitably lead to something else, still achieves its immediate effect upon us. We are, as it were, set off upon the trail at the end of this single sentence by the narrator's casual reference to a dozen particulars. Who are the squire, the doctor, and the "brown old seaman"? Where and what is Treasure Island and the treasure itself, both lifted and "not lifted"? Why does the tale begin with the advent of the seaman at the "Admiral Benbow"? At the same moment that Stevenson brings these questions to our attention, he plunges directly into the narrative that will provide the answers.

We have considered the passage from *Treasure Island* as an initial reminder that, although we shall be noting very different emphases in narrative fiction, the deliberate control of language which is fundamental to lyric poetry is equally vital in the writing of narrative prose. At the same time, we must realize that any accurate appreciation of the final purpose served by such a passage as this can come only with an understanding of the entire structure, of which this is the very beginning. As the aptness and effectiveness of single words in a lyric poem can only be assessed by the part they play in achieving the total poetic effect, so we know that our experience with a novel like *Treasure Island* amounts to far more than the scrutiny of single passages—however we may admire them.

To offer generalizations about narrative fiction is a precarious enterprise. Fiction takes infinite forms; the writers of it attempt an infinite number of things. There are obvious differences in what we can expect from a short story and from a novel of many hundreds of pages. It is, moreover, difficult to clarify our task by classifying fiction according to kinds. Although one can label narrative works according to such differentiae as length, subject matter, effect, or historical period, these categories themselves suggest very little about the actual construction of the works to which they are applied. Even so common a term as *novel* is remarkably difficult to define in an illuminating way, and literary historians who attempt to trace the development of the form continue to argue about precisely what works can be regarded as novels, and in what sense.

If, however, we adhere to our earlier assumption and approach narrative fiction, as we have poetry, in terms of its capacity to bring us pleasure, we should again be able to recognize the basic elements which are employed, in some proportion, in all narratives and which are the sources of their pleasurable effects. And, as was true of lyric poetry, the most obvious fact to be discovered in works of fiction is that they are *about* something, that their *substance* is their most conspicuous element. We observed that in some lyric poems, the substance could be regarded as a *plot*, while in others this term seemed difficult to apply. In narrative fiction, however, plot is almost always found in a conspicuous role. Indeed, we sometimes speak as though plot were synonymous with the work itself and, by referring to fictional works as "stories," we implicitly recognize that all other elements tend to be subordinate to the narration of events.

Plot is essentially the account of human activity, of significant changes from one state of human affairs to another. It is, in other words, the element in the work of fiction which is representative of men and women in *action*. Action, of course, need not be of an overt, physical kind. In fiction of an adult sort, indeed, action more often than not consists of the reflections, discoveries, decisions, and responses—the changes in knowledge and attitude and circumstances—which for most of us go to make up the shifting pattern of life itself.

To use the term *plot* profitably, we should agree that it need not necessarily refer to all of the occurrences which are recounted in a work of fiction. Indeed, it should be possible to reduce the plots of most narrative works—including many which are very long and elaborately written—to a summary sentence or two. This is, in effect, what we are likely to do when we are asked to describe the plot of a movie we have seen or a novel we have read; automatically we select the issues which have impressed us as crucial and the changes whereby they are resolved. Of course, no two people are likely to summarize a plot in exactly the same way; they may disagree over precisely which events should be included in the line of action which centrally focuses our interest and accounts for our ultimate response to the story.

Usually, however, we can agree upon the "beginning" of the plot. We recognize that, while a great deal of writing may be devoted to descriptions, conversations, and even occurrences which serve to inform us or cultivate our attitudes toward the world of the story, the plot properly may be said to begin with the emergence of some situation which calls for *resolution*. Through the discovery of an unanswered question or problem, the taking of a consequential action, the disclosure of a conflict, our attention is engaged and directed to a rather clearly sensed *issue*. We are led to anticipate change or action and, although we cannot predict its precise nature, we expect it to have relevance for, and ultimately to resolve in some fashion, the initial issue to which we have been introduced. Critics often speak, in rather elaborate ways, of the *unity*, or *coherence*, or *completeness* of plot, and it is true that in some complex literary works it is difficult to establish firmly the degree to which these qualities are present. Yet these are simply common-sense rules of storytelling, as we can see by considering how so simple a thing as an anecdote or "joke" is successfully narrated. For, obviously, the effective storyteller tells only one story at a time, he includes episodes and information which are relevant and no others, and he firmly concludes his tale with his "point," that surprise or discovery or situation which resolves and gives final meaning to whatever has preceded it.

In its relative simplicity, *Treasure Island* illustrates certain facts about plot to good advantage. Despite the length of the book, its plot can be summarized by saying that it concerns a group of people who seek for and ultimately discover hidden treasure. Such an assertion ignores the intricacy and ingenuity with which the plot is revealed to us and all of the episodes and conflicts which protract the process of treasure hunting, but it suggests the basic *kind* of action with which we are dealing and even implies that our final reaction to the work will be one of satisfaction over the discovery of what is being sought. The statement, moreover, indicates the principles of relevance which will set limits to the plot and govern the selection of incidents in its unfolding. The attainment of the treasure is the *end* of the action, not only because it terminates the plot but, in a broader sense, because it determines the kind of incident which will have relevance to the telling of this particular story.

Although we can establish significant facts about a plot by reducing it to such a blunt formula as we have that of *Treasure Island*, this procedure tells us little about the art by which the plot is actually revealed. To understand more about Stevenson's construction of plot, we should take into account the incidents through which it proceeds. An appropriate summary for this purpose might be somewhat as follows. An old buccaneer, who possesses the sole copy of a map indicating the hiding place of a large treasure, settles at the Admiral Benbow Inn on the English seacoast in order to hide from his former shipmates who desperately want the map. These pirates discover his whereabouts but are frustrated in their plans to get the map by the buccaneer's death and the fact that Jim Hawkins, the innkeeper's son, has himself taken the map. Jim's older friends, Dr. Livesey and Squire Trelawney, recognize the map for what it is and organize an expedition, which includes Jim, to recover the treasure from the island on which it is buried. The pirates, led by the sea-cook, John Silver, succeed in being hired as crew-members by the unsuspecting treasure seekers and plan, at the proper moment, to mutiny, kill Jim and his friends, and seize the treasure for themselves. Their plans are checked when Jim Hawkins accidentally overhears a revelatory conversation among them; and, when mutiny openly breaks out on the expedition's arrival at Treasure Island, Jim and his friends are prepared to offer vigorous resistance. Though out-numbered and besieged in a stockade on the island, the honest party refuses to come to terms with the mutineers. Jim is responsible for extricating his friends from their predicament, although more by good luck than anything else. In violation of orders, he twice deserts his companions to explore for himself. On the first of these adventures he encounters the maroon, Ben Gunn, who has actually dug up the treasure and is eager to ally himself with Jim and his comrades. On his second exploration, Jim is able to steal the ship from the pirates, who are guarding it in desultory, drunken fashion. But during this second absence from the stockade, Jim's friends have met with Gunn, learned the whereabouts of the treasure, and have accordingly surrendered the stockade and the now-useless map to the mutineers. Jim, unaware of this, returns to the stockade and falls into the hands of the mutineers who, upon their outraged discovery that the treasure has already been lifted, are prepared to kill both Jim and their deposed leader, John Silver. The two are rescued by Jim's comrades, who have been waiting in ambush. Leaving the surviving mutineers marooned on the island and accompanied by Silver (who ultimately steals away, never to be seen again), the expedition returns to England, laden with treasure.

This still very brief account of the action should reveal certain qualities of plot which explain some of the interest which *Treasure Island* has for most readers. Our suspense is basically awakened and sustained, as has been suggested, by the fact that the greater part of the book is the story of a *search;* the treasure, that is, exists as a goal, for the attainment of which we are hoping from the moment we learn of its existence. Equally important, however, is the presence in the latter part of the story of a *conflict,* a life-and-death struggle whose ultimate resolution we have no way of knowing but are naturally concerned to learn. As both search and conflict proceed, moreover, we encounter dramatic and usually unexpected changes, many of them so complete that they can be properly called *reversals.* When these occur, our expectations are shattered and our suspense is heightened by the sudden emergence of situations which surround Jim and his friends with new perils, problems, or opportunities. Some of these reversals occur directly as the result of actions which are depicted; of such a nature are the rescues, the outcomes of direct encounters in combat, the changes in fortune which we observe taking place as Jim battles the current in a small boat or matches wits and strength with the crafty pirate, Israel Hands, upon the deck of the *Hispaniola.*

More often than not, however, these reversals are accompanied by—and, in a sense brought about by—*discoveries.* The characters in the tale, and the reader along with them, are brought into the possession of knowledge which radically alters the appearance of their circumstances and prospects. For example, one of the most dramatic moments in *Treasure Island* involves little overt action. It is the famous scene in which, as the ship approaches the island, Jim crouches in an apple barrel on deck and learns of the villainous character and terrifying plans of his shipmates.

In I got bodily into the apple barrel, and found there was scarce an apple left; but, sitting down there in the dark, what with the sound of the waters and the rocking movement of the ship, I had either fallen asleep, or was on the point of doing so, when a heavy man sat down with rather a clash close by. The barrel shook as he leaned his shoulders against it, and I was just about to jump up when the man began to speak. It was Silver's voice, and before I had heard a dozen words, I would not have shown myself for all the world, but lay there, trembling and listening, in the extreme of fear and curiosity; for from these dozen words I understood that the lives of all the honest men on board depended on me alone.

The dozen words, of course, reveal that what has been regarded as an honest, high-spirited expedition is fatally threatened by a murderous conspiracy among the majority of its members—and what we have been regarding as the story of a voyage and search has become one of deadly conflict. This is only one of many passages in the book in which we find the characters, and especially Jim, moving from a state of ignorance or uncertainty to a knowledge which, as the case may be, is challenging, terrifying, or reassuring. Indeed, it is even possible to view the plot in terms of three major discoveries. The earliest section, despite its abundance of physical action, can be said to describe Jim's discovery of the old buccaneer's true identity and the significance of the map which he leaves behind him; the second section can be seen as terminating in the apple barrel scene, as Jim discovers the true character and villainous plans of the pirates who form the crew of the *Hispaniola;* and even the final section, with all of its combat and adventures by land and sea, moves toward and is ultimately resolved by discovery—not merely the discovery of the treasure but of the means, provided by Ben Gunn, by which it can be secured and the mutineers defeated.

Because *Treasure Island* is an adventure story for young readers, the discoveries it contains, while ingeniously conceived, are not very profound or complicated. In works of a more "intellectual" character, we are likely to encounter discoveries which are more subtle, and the passing from ignorance to knowledge, as we shall shortly point out in greater detail, may require our pursuing ideas and rational procedures of considerable complexity and, perhaps, of considerable intrinsic interest. In most of such works, however, the discovery can still be seen as a central element in the plot; it continues to constitute the action, the significant change which is the major object of our attention.

The obvious importance of discovery in most works of narrative fiction suggests certain formidable problems which confront the writer. Let us assume that an author has devised a plot in which, like the plot of *Treasure Island*, there are conflicts, reversals of fortune, and discoveries which seem calculated to produce in the reader feelings of suspense, anticipation, surprise, and ultimate satisfaction over an appropriate resolution. It is clear that the mere conception of plot and incident is only the beginning of his task. His story must be told, his plot unfolded, in a way which provides for the *reader* himself a continuing process of significant discovery. At the same time, although the plot may proceed in a way which the reader finds surprising or unusual, he must find its incidents entirely intelligible and, above all, *credible*. The plot of *Treasure Island* concludes with Jim's rescue by his friends at a moment when it appears that the treasure is lost and his life is about to be taken. This nick-of-time resolution is an agreeable surprise, but (unlike similar incidents in many cheap thrillers) it seems reasonable and believable because of episodes which have preceded it and information which is already in the possession of the reader. Stevenson's successful treatment of this incident is the consequence of certain fundamental decisions which, in common with all writers of narrative fiction, he has been forced to make.

Among the most important of such decisions is that involving what is frequently called *point of view*. Essentially, point of view may be described by answering the question "How much can the narrator be assumed to know?" And upon this answer rests the extent to which the reader, in turn, will be able to share the knowledge of the author and his characters.

There are a number of ways of categorizing and describing the possible points of view which are open to the writer of fiction. Certainly one of the most basic choices is between the use of the *first-person* or the *third-person* mode of narration. In a first-person narrative like *Treasure Island*, the tale purports to be a literal account, written or spoken by a fictional "I." In such a story we are presumably able to learn only what has been experienced—that is, undergone, observed, or learned—by the narrator, himself to some extent a character within the tale. In the narrative related in the third person entirely, the identity of the narrator is not recognized and the account ordinarily purports to be given with the impersonality of a factual newspaper story.

Within the two general classes suggested by first-person and third-person narrative, however, almost infinite diversity is possible. In the use of the first person, the precise role assumed by the narrator can vary enormously. Thus we have narrators who, like Jim Hawkins or Huckleberry Finn or David Copperfield, are clearly the principal figures in their own stories. Or we may have a narrator like Dr. Watson of the Sherlock Holmes tales, who plays a regular but subordinate role in the events he describes. And still again, there is the narrator who largely remains a kind of chronicler, with little stake save curiosity in the events which he purports to observe or hear about.

Among third-person narratives, the most important distinctions have to do with the kinds and quantity of information which, it is assumed, are accessible to the impersonal author. In many works, for example, the point of view can be described as *objective* or *external,* in the sense that nothing is reported which could not have been literally heard or seen by a non-participating observer. In such works, whatever insight we gain into the unspoken intellectual and emotional activities of the characters must be, as it is in life, inferred from their overt words and deeds; the author has, as it were, limited his function to that of a sound movie camera—although, like the director who employs such a camera, he can exercise great imagination in the choice of what he wishes to record.

At the opposite extreme from the objective point of view is that which is often called the *omniscient.* Here the author has access to the unspoken reflections and motivations of his characters; he is able to penetrate at will to their thoughts and emotions and, in fact, to describe, if he chooses, psychological forces operative upon characters who remain unaware of them. While it is this access to the inner experience of his characters which most significantly marks the omniscient narrator, he often assumes as well a knowledge of events and phenomena which, although unknown to any of the characters of the story, have some bearing upon their actions.

More often than not, the omniscience which an author assumes is to some extent "limited." The author, that is, may permit himself to enter the interior life of a single character, reporting upon the external activities of the others. Occasionally he may extend his insight into two or more characters but retain his objective point of view toward the rest. Where omniscience is limited to a single character, the effect is likely to be rather similar to that of first-person narration, for this approach seems to invite us to pursue the plot through the experiences and responses of only one of its participants.

While point of view determines a great deal about the total quality of a work of fiction, we must be circumspect in applying descriptive labels—those suggested above or any others—to any particular work. There are many novels in which, perceptibly or otherwise, points of view may shift. A narrative may begin as a first-person reminiscence and then, as in Flaubert's *Madame Bovary*, the narrator may lose all identity and become an impersonal but knowing reporter. On the other hand, many tales which are ostensibly told in the third person rely so heavily upon extended narrative speeches or writings by their characters that in effect they become largely first person in their point of view. Again, many authors, usually for sound artistic reasons, vary the degree of insight they permit themselves within a single work, sustaining, perhaps, an objective point of view save for certain crucial passages or alternating between reportorial accounts of what can be heard and seen and sections which frankly probe the reasonings and feelings of various characters. There are, moreover, kinds of narration which defy the categories into which points of view are traditionally placed. These include the "epistolary" novel or story, which takes the form of journal entries or correspondence among the various characters of the work. And there are authors like Fielding and Thackeray, who suspend the process of a third-person narrative at times in order to appear in their own historical identities for purposes of digression and comment. Certain novels of our own century, moreover, are even more difficult to discuss in terms of point of view; Joyce's *Ulysses*, for example, has its moments of conventional third-person narrative, but in his effort to probe the unarticulated feelings and thoughts of his characters, Joyce provides as well a totally unclassifiable amalgam of dramatic dialogue, past memories, present visual impressions, reflections and questions by a nameless author, unspoken internal soliloquies, parodies of other books, and literally dozens of other devices which prevent any generalizations whatever about the supposed narrator of the work.

But whatever the difficulty of describing an author's point of view, the fact remains that, for any given narrative moment, he must choose one and that, with this choice, he is making commitments, and facing limitations and opportunities. Thus in *Treasure Island* we know that, initially at least, Stevenson has chosen to tell his story as though it were being retrospectively set down by its boy hero. This point of view has obvious advantages, not the least of which is the sense of closeness, of "reality," which comes from the illusion that we are following an authentic document. Because Jim is the central figure of the events he describes and because he is an alert lad, we could not, it seems, learn the story from a better source. More important, as we have suggested, since Jim's own discoveries play such an important part in the plot, we are at most points sharing them—sharing the ignorance, curiosity, or bewilderment which precedes them and the surprise, fear, delight, and other emotions which they produce. In addition, we are spared in Jim's narrative the kind of details which an impersonal—and hence perhaps less selective—account might be expected to provide. Jim's adventurous young mind is, we might say, the ideal filter for the purpose of providing an adventure story; incidents and data which a more thoughtful or mature narration might have included are cheerfully neglected in favor of "high points" of excitement and suspense.

Although we may applaud Stevenson's choice of point of view, we must note certain limitations which it imposes upon him. His plot requires that certain critical events occur without the participation of Jim. In most places, we learn of these events as they are narrated to Jim by other characters—and indeed, such narrations form the discovery which we share with Jim. In one instance, however, it is desirable that we know in considerable detail of two concurrent lines of action; we are anxious to follow the course of open conflict which has broken out between our friends and the mutineers, but Jim, our narrator, has wandered away in search of his own adventures. Here Stevenson solves his problem by boldly changing the identity of his narrator and inserting the three chapters headed "Narrative Continued by the Doctor." There are other, similar limitations to what can be achieved by first-person narration, not the least of which is that the explicit insights we achieve into characters, situations, and events must be those of which our narrator seems to be capable. Jim Hawkins, for example, rarely provides more than a superficial, although lively, description of his friends and foes; the doctor, the squire, John Silver, and the others emerge in full stature largely because of inferences we are able to draw from what they say and do.

Clearly, however, the choice of point of view, like all of the choices an author must make, is governed entirely by the nature of the particular work he is creating and the effect he is seeking to produce upon his readers. *Treasure Island*, as Stevenson tells us in his introductory verses, is an old-fashioned adventure story for which the sharp-eyed, courageous, but rather unreflective Jim is an admirable choice of narrator. He is in sharp contrast, however, with such a figure as Marlow, the mature, widely experienced, and inquisitive narrator of many of Joseph Conrad's novels, which, though they too are, in a sense, tales of adventure at sea, involve profound and elusive issues of human conduct and belief.

Point of view represents only one of the many decisions which an author faces, once he has determined the general outline of his plot. Another formidable problem has to do with the *selection* of incident. Most narrative fiction of any length proceeds by a series of episodes. In many works, each episode can be seen as an advance in the plot, as a change which marks a stage in the total action. At the same time, however, we often are presented with episodes which serve other purposes. These may enlarge our understanding of character, heighten the various effects which the author seeks to create, provide information necessary to our understanding of the plot itself, or merely satisfy the reader's curiosity as to particulars—as when, for example, upon the conclusion of the principal action in *Treasure Island,* we learn briefly of the subsequent fortune of a few of the most colorful characters. But however "expendable" such episodes may seem in terms of the actual progress of the plot, they ordinarily have relevance for our understanding of and response to the story which is being told. The writer of fiction, unlike the historian or biographer, is compelled by no externally imposed standards to be comprehensive or just or conscientious; on the contrary, he is striving for effect, and this task alone provides the principle for the selection of incidents to be narrated. In consequence an entire sea-voyage may be summed up in a sentence, long periods of commonplace activity tacitly neglected, dozens of details cheerfully ignored. As readers in pursuit of the fictional action, we are willing to suspend most of the questions we would ordinarily ask in following the account of an authentic experience.

But, on the other hand, we demand that whatever episodes the author presents to us will sustain our interest in the story which he is committed to tell.

Treasure Island is notably economical in its inclusion of episodes which do not directly advance the action. As might be expected from an adventure story, the novel contains few scenes which do not directly represent the kind of conflict, discovery, or change in fortune which marks a direct step in the plot. Yet even in this tale, certain episodes are devoted to the establishment of mood or the revelation of character. There is, for example, the memorable scene in which Billy Bones, the arrogant buccaneer who has terrorized the visitors at the Admiral Benbow Inn, is rebuked by the impressive Dr. Livesey. Here we are introduced to the doctor and qualities of his character which will prove indispensable in later adventures; we gain a feeling, as well, of the terror engendered by the presence of an unprincipled and arrogant old pirate—a feeling which returns whenever, throughout the story, our hero is surrounded by men of Billy Bones's stamp. The episode would not be included in even a fairly detailed summary of the plot. Yet it serves—probably far better than any abstraction or analysis—to convey the kind of conflict we can anticipate when, life, death, and fortune at stake, pirates come face to face with honest men.

Another important consideration in the treatment of plot has to do with the *order* in which events are narrated. The author's decision in this respect is closely related to questions of discovery, for the *recognition* by characters and reader that certain events have taken place may often be more striking than the events themselves. While an ordinary chronological account of events seems the simplest principle of order and is probably the one most commonly encountered, it is surprising how frequently the events in a work of fiction are not narrated in the precise sequence in which they are supposed to have occurred. Even in *Treasure Island*, with its strictly chronological sequence of the adventures of Jim Hawkins, we and Jim learn only belatedly, through a narrative summary, of the circumstances under which Jim's companions have gained the treasure and the means for defeating their enemies. We are all familiar with the "flashback," in which the temporal sequence of the narration is abruptly suspended and we move back to events which occur, in time, prior to what we have regarded as the "beginning" of our story. Often this device is employed largely for expository reasons—to increase our understanding of or shape our attitudes toward the action which is recounted in conventional sequence. Just as often, however, the events revealed in this fashion are intrinsic to the central action. In these instances, the order of the plot does not coincide with the order of narration; the storyteller, as it were, does not begin at the beginning of his story. There is usually a good reason for this procedure. In some works of fiction—such, for instance, as many of Joseph Conrad's novels—we follow the piecing-together, by an inquiring narrator, of an action whose various episodes actually occur in an order very different from that in which they are learned about and told. And, as an extreme example of this sort of thing, there is the detective story in which, traditionally, the conclusion of the plot consists precisely in establishing and revealing the events which constitute its beginning.

In our discussion thus far we have tended to assume that each work of fiction possesses a single order of events which, whatever the mode or sequence of narration, may be summarized as one action. As a matter of fact, this can be said of most short stories, many plays, and a surprising number of longer novels. We must understand, however, that no ironclad rule insists that a work of narrative fiction contain only one, readily summarized plot. The reader can probably imagine kinds of work which resist such a mode of discussion: the novel in which we trace the activities of each of several characters, none of whom necessarily dominates the others as an object of interest; the novel which purports to deal with a number of events, occurring perhaps in a single setting or attributable to a common cause; the novel which consists of a series of relatively disassociated adventures, of which each, while occurring to one person or group of people, is substantially complete in itself. Fictional works of this kind—unless they frankly profess to be collections of some sort—ordinarily possess some clear principle which binds them together and invites us to regard them as unified. Such a principle may, as we shall shortly point out in greater detail, reside in something other than plot—in character, or in setting—but very often it is possible to isolate a "main" plot as well as subservient lines of action which augment its effect. Thus, for example, the actions of a hero may acquire greater clarity by contrast or comparison with those of a subordinate character; the nature and progress of one love affair may assume greater importance by virtue of its contrast with another. Or the central conflict within a single plot may be represented as the culmination of two autonomous lines of action, each of which traces the development, for example, of characters who are finally confronted with one another. Critical discussions of fictional works often use the term "subplot," implying by its employment that, while a central line of action can be discerned, there is also a subordinate action with some sort of demonstrable relationship to the principal line of the plot. Although we have said that no arbitrary rules govern the writing of narrative fiction, stories of any kind ordinarily are shaped by certain ous facts about our human capacity to apprehend, remen and remain interested. It seems only natural that, in rea fiction, we wish fully to understand and freely to respond "what happens." This is probably why, in even the most co plex narratives, we are usually able to discern a single, co plete line of action which is, as it were, the "story," the fou dation for the entire literary experience.

We have said that fiction represents *human beings* in action, and, while our emphasis has thus far been upon plot, we have had, at least tacitly, to recognize that any plot which has significance for us involves *character*. Now, when we speak of *characters*, we refer to the persons, the agents, who inevitably must undergo the experiences with which fiction concerns itself. Ordinarily, however, when we speak of *character* in a work of literary art, we speak of the qualities—moral, emotional, and intellectual—with which the agents have been endowed by the author. It is imperative that, to at least some extent, we know something of character, for action alone rarely has the power to elicit from us any clear response. We have suggested that *Treasure Island*, for example, represents an action of search and conflict. In pursuing the plot and considering its resolution, we must distinguish between Jim's companions and the pirates; our entire reaction depends, that is, upon Stevenson's making clear that the honest treasure hunters *are* honest and worthy of sympathy, while the mutineers are deplorable villains. Small children who, in watching television or the movies, are at pains to point out the "good guys" and "bad guys" are simply pursuing a fundamental distinction of character on which depends their entire satisfaction in the action they are following. The identical fall from a horse may be a matter of tragic distress, good-natured amusement, or savage elight, depending on whether it is the hero, the buffoon, or the villain who does the falling.

Even where the moral quality of the characters is by no means as clearly established as it is in the average adventure story—where, for example, the author deliberately introduces ambiguous or conflicting evidence of his hero's moral stature —our interpretation and judgment of the work must be colored inevitably by our feelings toward the human figures the author has set before us. Some readers, particularly in recent times, are likely to stress the psychological or emotional aspects of the human personality, to dismiss as naïve the distinction between good and bad characters, and to insist that moral assessments play little part in our response to a thoughtful work of adult fiction. It would seem, however, that aside from the occasional work of fiction which purports merely to present an "objective," clinical view of the human personality, we continue to judge fictional characters in terms which, if not those of conventional morality, imply clear degrees of sympathy or aversion. Psychological insights can alter our judgments or affect the language in which we express them, facts which many modern authors take into full account. In doing so, however, such writers continue to appeal very fundamentally to our capacities for admiration or disapproval, compassion or distaste—for from these proceed our responses to human affairs, in fiction as in life.

Characterization obviously demands more than the establishment of moral stature. Characters must be, among other things, *credible*. Most of us do not insist that the characters we encounter in fiction be "real," in the sense that we can find their precise counterparts in the world about us. We do ask, however, that they seem convincing, that we can believe in them sufficiently to be concerned about them and to anticipate in some fashion the way in which they will behave. Fictional characters can be unique—indeed, we tend to rejoice in whatever is uncommon about them—yet in their words and acts we expect a certain internal *consistency*. We ask that they remain "in character," that they retain an outline, however broad or wild, which the author has created for them. In the concluding pages of *Treasure Island*, John Silver moves in astonishing fashion through stages of prudent servility, masterful coolness, savage and murderous greed, honorable courage, good-natured resignation, and avaricious guile. This progression, unthinkable in the conduct of any sane man, does not tax our credulity, for it is entirely what can be expected from the cruel, cunning, yet perversely attractive old rogue, whose paradoxical portrait has emerged so clearly in the preceding incidents of the story.

Credible characters about whose moral nature we have no doubt can still be remarkably tedious. We tend to enjoy in our fictional as well as our real companions the company of diversified and colorful personalities. Rich characterization is a source of intrinsic interest—as well, it may be added, as an inducement to distinguish between and remember the agents of the story. In *Treasure Island*, despite the relative simplicity of the tale, we find a lively diversity of characterization. There is a broad and uncomplicated distinction between honest men and villains: we speedily see that the innkeeper's son, the squire, the doctor, and their friends abound in honesty and good faith, while the pirates are, ex officio, the blackest of knaves. But the characters who share common moral qualities are by no means cut from the same cloth in other respects: there is the urbane, gentle, but courageous doctor; the blustering but honest squire; the resolute and outspoken Captain Smollett; the stout-hearted but irresponsible Jim. And the pirates present a subtle gradation in villainy, from Pew, the

81

odious and terrifying blind beggar to the memorable Silver, the murderous turncoat who remains, with his warmth and wit, the obvious superior of his blackguard associates.

Thus far we have been discussing what might be regarded as the "product" of characterization—the impressions of character which the author manages to convey to his reader. To achieve this characterization, to provide the information which forms the basis for our estimate of character, is a task which writers of fiction undertake in many different ways. In one kind of story the author may be content directly to describe character—a procedure which, in itself, can range from the use of a few simple adjectives to the production of an elaborate, analytical study. In certain fictional works, generally of a rather superficial kind, the author may depend upon our preconceptions concerning certain "types," exploiting our assumptions that policemen or cowboys are "good guys" unless proved otherwise or that gamblers or sorcerers are disposed, by definition, to be morally despicable.

In most adult fiction, at least some of the characterization is achieved by less direct methods, and readers are invited to draw their own inferences from evidence provided in the course of the narrative. Characters emerge and affect us, each in his own way, largely because of what they themselves say and do, rather than because the author directly tells us about them. As in life, we learn about character in fiction chiefly from those situations in which it is openly displayed. It is difficult to feel certain that a man is generous unless his generosity is put to the test; we can say little about courage except where it is called into play. In a work of fiction, we tend to discover the moral qualities of characters by the *choices* they make. We believe in Jim Hawkins' bravery because he chooses the course which displays this quality in each of several dramatic situations; there is no facet of Silver's rather complex character which does not come to light because of a decision he makes or an action he undertakes. Character, in short, is inextricably involved with action, both because it is most clearly *manifested* through the actions in which men engage and because it *determines* the nature of those actions and, in turn, the attitudes with which we regard them.

In many works, *Treasure Island* among them, the account of events and actions is clearly the major source of our interest, and the delineation of character can be seen essentially as a way of shaping our response to plot. In such works, therefore, character is subordinate, though indispensable, to plot. Some works of fiction, however, tend to subordinate plot to character—to employ actions and events for the purpose of portraying the moral or intellectual qualities of a particular character or group of characters. Confronted with the major personality of such a work, the reader is not so much concerned with questions of what will happen to him as to what sort of person he really is. The plot—for whatever emphasis appears to dominate the story, there must be a plot of some sort—is not necessarily complete or unified because it represents a single and complete action, but it is adequate because whatever occurs provides a satisfactory account of character. It is difficult to prove that either plot or character is primary within a given narrative, for obviously the individual reader is free to determine what interests him most. It does appear, however, that there are works of fiction in which the plot represents an action that is fragmentary or unresolved, yet interesting and satisfying as a vehicle for the revelation of character. In such works, action of some sort is almost inevitably present, for we learn what people are from what they do, but the portrayal of character must be seen as the end and the organizing principle of the narrative.

Traditionally, a distinction is often made between *character* and *thought* in works of fiction, although it may be argued that since the latter represents the intellectual aspects of the human personality as the former does the moral or emotional, both serve the common end of "characterization." We can describe as thought whatever passages in a work disclose the reasoned deliberations, assertions, and decisions of the characters, and it is therefore true that to a considerable extent such passages can serve the purpose of characterization; intellectual habits, attitudes, and convictions are, like moral predispositions, constituents of character which condition human actions. Beyond this, however, the reflections, arguments, demonstrations, and conclusions which reflect thought are usually intrinsic to the action which is being represented. It is true that in John Silver's debates with his enemies or his rascally companions we find abundant evidence of his cunning, colorful, and perversely attractive mind. More importantly, however, he is exercising his intellectual gifts in actions, the success or failure of which have clear consequences for the future course of events within the plot.

Thought, therefore, is rarely a static element, a gratuitous introduction of intellectual analysis in which the reflective character stands, as it were, aloof from the action. Nor is it, on the other hand, the "author's thought," the message or moral which has to be inferred from the narrative. It is, rather, the representation of intellectual action which, as action, can form part—or indeed the whole—of the narrative plot. Few works of mature fiction fail to rely substantially upon thought, for the occurrences in such works tend to follow not from mere accident or moral predisposition alone, but from the kinds of deliberate reflections and judgments of which man, as a rational creature, is capable.

Even though we recognize the integral relationship between

thought and action, the intellectual ingredient in a work of fiction may exercise its own, relatively independent, appeal. Important ideas, original insights, and displays of intellectual power all have their own capacity to attract us, whether they appear in the spoken words or the internal reflections which are attributed to fictional characters. Certain great works of fiction are conspicuously "philosophic," not because we are supposed to infer various significant general propositions from the particular events of the narrative, but because they provide overtly, in speeches and the other ways in which thought is revealed, an account of valuable, systematic deliberation about questions which are themselves authentic and important.

Unlike character, thought does not appear capable of transcending plot as the main organizing principle in a genuine work of narrative fiction. There are obviously stories in which, while plot is primary, the action it represents is predominantly and even exclusively intellectual. In a sense, certain detective stories are of this sort. Our chief satisfaction is derived not from observing the defeat of evil or the restoration of justice but from following and admiring the intellectual virtuosity with which a Sherlock Holmes or Hercule Poirot employs his powers of reasoning to move from ignorance to knowledge, carrying us with him as he goes. There are, as well, more subtle stories of "discovery," in which what is found is not buried treasure or the identity of a fictitious murderer, but some significant truth, possessing inherent interest in terms of questions which exist quite outside the work of fiction. Of such a sort, for example, are many "biographical" novels in which we trace the intellectual growth of a hero and observe the display of his intelligence as it encounters problems which we ourselves believe to be urgent and authentic.

When, however, we encounter a work in which narrative

seems to exist only as a vehicle for conveying a doctrine whose truth and importance are presumably to strike us with their own independent force, we have, it may be argued, gone beyond the limits of the storyteller's art, and indeed of imaginative literature in general. Philosophic dialogues, moral allegories, various religious or political tracts, and "case histories" of all kinds may rely on fictions, to be sure, but they are fictions which have been introduced in the service of the philosopher, teacher, journalist, or rhetorician, rather than of the storyteller. There is no reason why the thought in a narrative work should not provide valuable stimulation, instruction, and persuasion with respect to questions that are very important and very real. But the art of fiction ultimately preserves its identity among the many uses of language by the fact that it deliberately departs from literal reality, that it is an art of imaginative creation with the production of delight as its final purpose.

In most narrative works, a great preponderance of what is written can be related directly to the representation of plot or of the various aspects of character. In addition, however, narrative actions occur in time and place, and writers of fiction, accordingly, devote some attention as a rule to what is usually called *setting*. The sense of setting can be conveyed in many ways and can assume widely varying degrees of importance. For example, literal and direct physical description can be provided merely to clarify the precise nature of certain actions, to establish, as it were, a map which enhances the reader's understanding of where and how certain actions occur. On the other hand, eloquent physical description can, like certain lyric poems, enable us through its imagery to sense and participate vicariously in the experience offered by particular settings. Usually the power to convey such impressions is employed to augment the general effect of the action; Treasure Island, with its alien animal and vegetable life, its unhealthy smells, its forbidding coast and sinister swamps, is a setting which enhances our apprehensiveness over the fate of those who land there. The settings of narratives, furthermore, can be established in ways other than literal description. These include the apparently casual references, woven into the narrative, from which we can piece together the image of a particular place at a particular time. Thus, again in *Treasure Island*, the allusions to historic sailors and pirates, the mounted revenue officers and lumbering stagecoaches, the fleeting glimpses of a manorial park, a rural hamlet, an isolated inn, or a busy sailing town all combine to provide us with the flavor of maritime England's coast in the early eighteenth century.

Setting, however, can include less tangible elements than physical appearance or even, for that matter, customs and institutions. For environment is a matter, among other things, of prevailing beliefs, habits, and values—moral and intellectual as well as social. Even, once again, in *Treasure Island*, we sense, through the casual talk of keelhauling and of bloody deeds, through the coarse and morbid character of frivolous songs and stories, through the blasphemy of common conversation, and through the readiness of even honest men to act violently and unreflectively, that our story is set in a time when life was active and precarious and when physical combat and violent death were taken as a matter of course.

Especially if we consider it in its broadest sense, setting can do more than provide background to action or augment the effect which the action achieves. It can be employed, almost literally, as an agent, as a force which affirmatively determines the course of the action. *Treasure Island*, after all, derives its name from its setting, and a major factor in the action is the threat of starvation, disease, and abandonment imposed by the isolation and inhospitable climate of the island. In many other narratives, setting in its broader and less concrete aspects plays an even more prominent part; we are all familiar with the fictional struggle between the individual and an environment which, in its attitudes, values, or circumstances, operates as a hostile force. Indeed, it is possible to imagine—although rather difficult to find—works in which setting serves as the dominant and organizing element and in which the author, without attempting genuine historical reconstruction, employs his characters and their actions for the ultimate purpose of creating within us a sense of a real or fictional place and period.

The "writing" of fiction obviously involves powers of conception, of selection, of construction. Plot, character, and thought can presumably be "imagined" by an author before he sets a word upon paper. But obviously, when these decisions have been made, the art of fiction depends as indispensably as does poetry upon language itself—upon the *diction* which alone brings before us the product of the author's imagination and judgment. Thus, as we pointed out at the beginning of this chapter, the narrative writer faces problems which differ in degree rather than in kind from those which confront writers of other sorts of imaginative literature. Yet it would be false to assert that while the difference between narrative prose and lyric poetry is one of emphasis, it is not ordinarily very great. It is true that the conscientious novelist or short-story writer will lavish great care upon the selection of individual words and phrases. It is also true that in many works of fiction, the resources of imagery, of connotation, of symbolism, and even of sound are conspicuously exploited—so that, for example, passages and even entire works impress us as substantially "poetic" by virtue of the power which the language itself exerts. At the same time, as we have already asserted, the *substance* dominates virtually all works of fiction. Only very rarely do we find a narrative work in which the substance—the plot or character—serve, as they often do in poetry, as a mere mode of organization, an "excuse" for the introduction of language which achieves the principal effect of the work. In practice, it is difficult, although not impossible, to isolate within a work of prose fiction the passage which does not contribute to plot, character, thought, or setting. Thus, although the diction in our opening passage from *Treasure Island* has certain qualities which may be independently attractive, the great achievement of this paragraph can be assessed only when we view it as an instrument of the storyteller, as a means by which we learn about and become interested in the people and the actions which are what *Treasure Island* is "about." In narrative fiction we ask of language primarily that it reveal the substance; we may rejoice in its intrinsic power to please us, but ultimately we expect from it a clarity, aptness, and credibility which will do justice to the human actions which are being represented.

There is one species of literature in which the resources of language and the charm of narrative can be exploited in equal measure. This, of course, is *narrative poetry*. The union of narrative and linguistic power appears to finest advantage in true *epic poems*, those lengthy metrical narrations in which early and fundamental qualities of a civilization or religion are revealed through men and deeds, alike heroic in stature. The great length of the epic permits a plot which is somewhat looser in its unity than those in shorter works, yet is bound together by the presence of a central figure or a comprehensive conflict or issue. Within the Homeric epics, for example, we can discern the same elements of plot, character, thought, and setting which characterize conventional works of prose fiction, and, indeed, the effect of these narratives is clear, even when they are translated into modern English prose. At the same time we can sense, even in most prose translations, the epic poet's dependence on the significative power of language; for the impression of vast and unqualified magnitude, which is one of the great hallmarks of the epic poem, continues to be vigorously conveyed through the images and figures which survive in translation. If, moreover, we wish to see how metrical writing and the musical force of language blend inextricably with meaning and with all the elements of narrative, we have only to consider Milton's *Paradise Lost*, the great English epic, in which narrative, doctrine, and diction seem equally to account for the grandeur of the poem.

In certain other, less ambitious kinds of narrative poetry the resources of the narrative writer and the lyric poet also seem to be employed in almost equal proportion. This is the case in some, although by no means all, ballads—*folk ballads* (of unknown but presumably spontaneous or informal origin) as well as *literary ballads* (deliberately constructed by a single, identified author). Since ballads are presumably written to be sung, they tend to display a very genuine lyrical quality, often attributable in part to repetition of various kinds. At the same time, many of them, including folk ballads, are marked by an ingenuity of plot and of narrative technique which produces effects very similar to those of certain short stories.

We must not be led, however, by the presence of metrical and other lyrical elements in narrative verse to assume that it inevitably represents the perfect union of substance and diction. In most narrative poems, as in other kinds of literary works, an emphasis is apparent, and though each of several elements may make a conspicuous contribution to the total effect of the work, we can usually discern some principle which orders the whole and is the primary source of our response. And if we are rigorous in applying the term "narrative" to poetry, we should do so only with those works in which storytelling is paramount. Such other effects as the experiencing of mood, the gaining of insight or conviction, or the mere enjoyment of the powers of language—all of which are appropriate to other literary kinds—only subserve the principal effect of the narrative art. And that effect is achieved through representing the actions and the affairs of men.

This is perhaps what has led some students of literature to place considerable emphasis upon what is often called *theme* in narrative works. The term is usually employed to describe a topic or problem which is found in the action and which seems both authentic and significant in our own experience with the world of reality. To state the theme of a story is to generalize upon the particulars of the narrative, to place upon the fictional characters in their fictional situations the classifications we apply to genuine human experience. It is, as well, to stress similitudes between what appears within the fictional narrative and what appears significantly within life itself. Thus, for example, we spoke of the plot of *Treasure Island* as fundamentally one of search, complicated by conflict. We might employ virtually the same terms in describing the "theme" of the work, pointing out, for example, that Jim's adventures embody a perennial youthful dream of travel, conflict, and ultimate reward, or that *Treasure Island* is the youngster's ideal image of a romantic escape from the commonplace. Somewhat more satisfactorily we could no doubt establish a number of themes in a novel like *Huckleberry Finn:* the conflict of primitive good will and common sense with the arbitrary authority and prejudice of society; the conflict between freedom and restraint; the human illusion that the romantic is the remote and inaccessible; the divinity of nature, as manifested in the godlike quality of a mighty river and contrasted to the frail, ephemeral quality of human affairs.

Discussions of theme in works of fiction may very well illuminate—and perhaps augment—some of the appeal which stories have for us. When we describe the theme of a novel, we tend to suggest that it involves problems and situations which are familiar and meaningful and in which we have, so to speak, a vested interest and can therefore view with real sympathy the affairs of the fictional characters. Emphasis upon theme may also suggest that the work of fiction provides comment or insight or data, to be filed away, with whatever else we have gained from whatever source, under "social conflict," "unrequited love," "youthful imagination," and such other categories as are involved in our definition of theme. It is this latter fact which suggests that we exercise a certain restraint in our pursuit of theme. It is certainly useful to recognize that important problems, familiar situations, and universal human traits are represented in a work of fiction. But the importance, familiarity, or even the universality of what a novel represents are not its ultimate reason for existence. Its distinctive capacity—as distinguished from those of many other kinds of literature—is to bring us a pleasure which, depending on the nature of the work, may be of many different sorts. And, while it is conceivable that this pleasure may genuinely proceed from the recognition of what is universally urgent or true within the fictional situation, it is far more likely to involve one or more of the diversified but outright emotions which the true storyteller seeks to produce. The great storytellers ask, to be sure, for our alertness, compassion, and imagination, but, in return, their ultimate gift is a pleasurable one. The true "universality" of fiction does not lie in the breadth or importance of its themes, but in its unfailing power to delight thoughtful men in all places and at all times.

3

READING DRAMATIC
LITERATURE

In this chapter we shall be chiefly concerned with qualities which are peculiar to the drama. We shall, that is, be noting characteristics of plays which are found neither in lyric poetry nor in narrative fiction and which are largely attributable to the fact that drama, unlike other kinds of literature, is written to be performed—and hence is largely dependent upon the overt words and actions of actors, representing its characters, for the achievement of much of its artistic effect.

At the outset, however, we should again remind ourselves that all of the arts which employ language to bring pleasure to the reader or spectator have a great deal in common. The dramatist, like the writers of all imaginative literature, finds in language more than a medium of communication whereby whatever may be defined as the substance of his work is disclosed; he exploits, in addition, the powers of meaning and sound by which, as we have pointed out, language provides its own aesthetic satisfactions to an audience. While our emphasis in this chapter will be upon problems which uniquely confront the dramatist, we shall urge accordingly that the student remain aware of the presence, in most dramatic works, of those qualities of structure, imagery, and sheer verbal music which he has learned to associate with lyric verse.

There are, moreover, additional interesting similarities between the procedures of the playwright and those of the lyric poet. In the drama, as in the genuine lyric, for example, the "official" identity of the author disappears and the language becomes entirely that of a "speaker," whose personality may or may not coincide with that of the actual writer of the work. In this respect, indeed, most lyric poems have their dramatic elements, for it is possible to regard them as speeches, produced by a fictional character within some kind of implicit imaginative situation. Thus each of the three poems which we considered in our first chapter can be viewed as statements produced with respect to certain deliberately constructed situations and reflecting facts, attitudes, and thoughts which—whatever the extent to which they coincide with the views of the historically authentic author of the poem—are those of a "speaker" whose identity is defined only in terms of the work itself. Conversely, individual speeches within a dramatic work often yield to the same kind of discussion as does a single lyric poem. Frequently, in fact, a single speech within a play can be regarded as an autonomous poetic construction, and, as we all know, certain famous dramatic passages are cherished for essentially the same reasons as are genuine lyric verses. For in many sustained dramatic speeches, the playwright shares with the lyric poet the problem of assuming the identity of a fictional character and employing language to do full justice to an explicit or implicit fictional situation which, if properly represented, has the power to move an audience in certain rather definite ways.

The relationship between drama and narrative fiction, on the other hand, is equally important. It is clear that the playwright, although he cannot, like the narrative writer, openly appear as a storyteller, has a story which must be told. In consequence, much of what has been said about the elements of narrative literature applies equally well to the drama. The playwright's task, like that of the narrative writer, is the representation of human actions and accordingly it is his *plot* which, more often than not, provides the organizing principle of the drama and is the major source of its effect. Indeed, as we shall point out in greater detail, the limited scope within which the dramatist works tends to give his writing a special "plotfulness," for the economy which the dramatic manner imposes upon the author discourages the inclusion of speeches and episodes which do not bear rather clearly upon the development of the action, which is generally the play's reason for existing.

Character, too, whatever means the playwright may peculiarly employ for its representation, serves in drama the same fundamental purpose as it does in narrative fiction. For our responses to the representation of human action continue to be governed by constant psychological and moral principles, whatever the literary mode which presents them to us, and our basic reactions to a given character remain the same, whether he is described to us by a narrator or impersonated by an actor. In drama, moreover, since we are rarely confronted with the overt comments of the author, the term *thought* can be seen with particular clarity as a description of the intellectual procedures of the characters as they emerge in dialogue.

Setting, although it appears in the drama in a number of special ways, can serve the same diversity of purposes for which it is employed by the novelist or short-story writer. And those who regard the presence of an authentic topic, problem, or theme as an important ingredient in imaginative literature can find what they seek as readily in plays as in short stories or novels. In effect, then, the same literary elements which we have discerned in fiction can be found in any sort of "story," whether or not we particularly note the manner—narrative or dramatic—in which it is presented. Novels can be, and often are, "adapted" for the stage or screen or broadcast, while dramatic plots can be readily recounted in narrative form. In either case, we generally regard the "adaptation" as successful if the formal elements remain substantially unaltered, if the plot, character, thought, and setting remain constant to both versions—if, that is, what we tend to think of as the "story" remains the same.

These similarities among literary kinds are of considerable importance, for they suggest that any imaginative writer, whatever expertness he has achieved in the creation of particular forms, must produce works in which arresting ideas and activities are effectively represented by language. And they imply as well that certain kinds of fundamental alertness, sympathy, and sensitivity govern our responses to all imaginative literary works, regardless of the form and the circumstances in which they reach us. It is obvious, nonetheless, that the playwright's procedures can be distinguished from those of the novelist or poet by certain limitations and opportunities with which the dramatic manner of representation confronts him. And particularly in the reading of plays, which are almost always intended for performance, we must exercise patience and imagination, recognizing that the printed version of a dramatic work, while it can usually provide us with the most central and valuable qualities of literary experience, is in some sense a preliminary to the actual theatrical production, to the finished performance, which is, as a rule, the playwright's goal. We, the readers, are invited to share with the playwright the final prospect of theatrical production, a prospect which accounts for most of the significant distinctions between the works of the narrative and the dramatic writer.

Since we shall be conducting our discussion of these distinctions in rather general terms throughout most of this chapter, it may be well to remind ourselves that they are, nonetheless, thoroughly practical ones. For what finally appears as a play is, as often as not, initially conceived of as simply a "story," in which, however carefully constructed the plot or thoroughly visualized the characters, there is very little which specifically requires either narrative or dramatic manner of presentation. When, however, the actual process of dramatic creation begins —when, that is, the "story" is embodied in a *play*—we must anticipate many changes and developments. Some of these are the obvious and necessary consequences of the author's choice of the dramatic manner and represent the inevitable conversion of narrative material into dialogue, but others represent decisions made voluntarily and thoughtfully by the playwright in an effort to exploit the opportunities of dramatic form.

The examination of almost any story which is available in both dramatic and narrative form should reveal many of the important differences between the two kinds of literary art. Let us consider very briefly the use made by Shakespeare of a "borrowed" story in *Romeo and Juliet*. In its most rudimentary form, this tale of a tragic love between the members of two hostile families can be traced back to the Middle Ages, and, in most of its major details, it appears in an Italian story— subsequently adapted and translated in other languages—almost seventy-five years before the first publication of Shakespeare's play. Abundant evidence, however, suggests that Shakespeare used as his direct source Arthur Brooke's *Romeus and Juliet*, a long narrative poem which was first published in 1562. The two works are fairly comparable in length, since Brooke's poem is over three thousand lines long, and they coincide very closely in the structure of the central plot; indeed, a detailed summary of the ill-fated love affair as it appears in Brooke would apply with considerable accuracy to Shakespeare's play. Let us ask ourselves what important differences can be found between the two works, suspending any judgment concerning the relative excellence of the two treatments and seeking only those changes in the play which can be attributed, in some degree, to Shakespeare's use of the dramatic manner.

Even the most superficial comparison of the two works will reveal those changes which were *necessary* in adapting the narrative for the theater. Almost all of these can be attributed to the necessary suppression of the narrator—to the fact that whatever is described or recounted in the poem must become known from the speeches and actions of characters within the play. Sometimes this is achieved in obvious and very simple ways. Brooke, for example, devotes a hundred lines to describing Romeo's disconsolate, extravagant, and unrequited love for Rosaline, and, although this lengthy passage includes an exchange of speeches between Romeo and his sensible (and here unnamed) friends, the history of this passion, in its various stages and over a period of several months, is traced by means of a detailed narrative account. Shakespeare, on the other hand, provides his account of Romeo's "preliminary" romance in ways suitable to the drama. First, in the description provided by another character, namely Benvolio, he is able, almost in the same fashion as the narrative writer, to suggest the continuing, habitual aspects of Romeo's love and in such lines as

> Many a morning hath he there been seen,
> With tears augmenting the fresh morning's dew,
> Adding to clouds more clouds with his deep sighs . . .

he conveys a clear account of behavior which is, so to speak, chronic. Then, since the current, acute moment of Romeo's unrequited love is rather specifically related to the plot—it prompts him, in the play, to attend the Capulet feast—Shakespeare introduces Romeo himself to reveal, through his own words and gestures, the stage which he has reached in his unhappy passion.

Such a comparison as the foregoing represents one of many points in the play at which Shakespeare has retained descriptions and incidents in the narrative work by devices which, while brilliant in the details of their execution, involve little more than the "translation" into dramatic dialogue of materials originally presented by a third-person narrator, himself dependent on direct quotation to some extent. Far more arresting are those places in which Shakespeare, faced with the same fundamental problem of incorporating within the form of his drama the elements of the story, exploits the challenge which confronts him for the construction of novel and unforgettable, yet entirely relevant, speeches, episodes, and characters. The product of this fertile and original response to the challenge of the drama is conspicuously evident when we compare the ways in which Brooke and Shakespeare represent the feud between the Capulets and the Montagues. Space does not permit our examining in detail the way in which, in *Romeo and Juliet*, the feud recurrently and vividly appears in many aspects, not only as a basic force within the plot but as a kind of pervasive background, which, in its harsh, unlovely violence, sets off to superb advantage the warm poignancy of the love affair. Brooke's treatment of the feud, on the other hand, can be described by saying that, save for a few passages where it is briefly though piously deplored, he is concerned with the state of affairs in Verona only to the extent that it directly affects the fate of the lovers.

It is worth devoting a few moments, however, to a comparison of the ways in which the narrative poet and the playwright initially convey the facts which we need in order to understand the background of strife which precipitates the tragedy. Brooke, after naming the Capulets and Montagues as ancient families of Verona, describes the feud in these lines:

A wonted use it is, that men of likely sort,
(I wot not by what fury forced) envy each other's port.
So these, whose egall state bred envy pale of hue,
And then, of grudging envy's root, black hate and rancour grew.
As, of a little spark, oft riseth mighty fire,
So of a kindled spark of grudge, in flames flash out their ire:
And then their deadly food, first hatched of trifling strife,
Did bathe in blood of smarting wounds; it reaved breath and life,
No legend lie I tell, scarce yet their eyes be dry,
That did behold the grisly sight, with wet and weeping eye.
But when the prudent prince, who there the sceptre held,
So great a new disorder in his commonweal beheld;
By gentle mean he sought, their choler to assuage;
And by persuasion to appease, their blameful furious rage
But both his words and time, the prince hath spent in vain:
So rooted was the inward hate, he lost his busy pain.
When friendly sage advice, ne gentle words avail,
By thund'ring threats, and princely power their courage 'gan he quail.
In hope that when he had the wasting flame suprest,
In time he should quite quench the sparks that burned within their breast.

In this passage, despite its archaic appearance to modern readers, Brooke employs to excellent advantage the resources of both narrative and lyric which are available to the narrative poet. To his account of the origin and growth of the feud, Shakespeare, from the standpoint of specific facts, adds little. Brooke, moreover, brings us skilfully to the stage of temporarily arrested hostility at which the Romeo and Juliet tale begins and in which we recognize a condition in which, as Brooke subsequently says, each enemy "with outward friendly show doth hide his inward state." This artfully developed nar-

100

ration, in addition, is presented with a good deal of ingenious metaphor which presents the feud as a smoldering, sinister, and lamentable affair from which no very cheerful outcome can possibly be expected. We should note, as well, the "personal appearance" of the narrator who becomes, with his professions of ignorance and honesty, a sort of fictional character in his own right.

Brooke, in short, in the manner of the narrative poet, has provided us with information and suggested attitudes which we should take toward it. There is no reason why an author seeking to embody the same situation in a drama should strive to do more. Let us remind ourselves, however, of the way in which the history and current character of the feud become known in *Romeo and Juliet*. We recall that the first 120 lines or so of the play's opening scene are devoted to a "manifestation" of the feud, an outcropping of the bitter hostility which, at one and the same time, reveals the character of the situation and culminates in the Prince's threat of death against those who continue overt warfare—the same threat which has such direct consequences for the principal action of the play. In this scene, that is, we not only learn the nature of the feud but, as in Brooke's poem, learn of its most current development in an incident which is, at the very least, an indispensable antecedent to the plot itself.

In this instance, however, Shakespeare has done far more than "adapt" the narrative account of Brooke by converting it into appropriate dramatic dialogue. He has created a new, elaborate, and immensely lively scene, in which, through the highly particular responses of particular men in a particular place, the general situation emerges with total clarity. The hovering presence of the feud initially is felt through the bawdy and irresponsible quarrel of the serving men who, even in their coarse exchanges, suggest the scope of an enmity which lies "between our masters and us their men." In the crescendo of activity which follows, the battle is joined first by the noble younger members of the feuding families, then by "several of both houses" who swell the numbers of the combatants, next by citizens and officers seeking to restore peace yet only adding to the violence of the scene, and finally by the ancient heads of the warring houses who, in their fierce threats and manifest frailty, provide a sort of climactic paradox, typifying all that is grotesque and unreasonable in the affair. In its trivial inception, its onrushing development and growth, and its ultimate blaze of fury, the encounter has a good deal of resemblance to the fire with which Brooke metaphorically compares the entire feud. And, as the outraged Prince restores the peace with his threats (and at the same time presents an excellent summary of the history of the feud), we feel, much as we did in reading Brooke, that the flame, temporarily suppressed, will continue to smolder and will doubtless break out anew with tragic consequences.

In this scene Shakespeare has achieved most of the ends attained by the passage from Brooke, for, as we have suggested, he has conveyed a rather comprehensive view of the feud and displayed, in all its vigorous immediacy, the incident which is to have such tragic ultimate consequences for the love of Romeo and Juliet. He has, however, accomplished this almost entirely by the representation of *particulars*, of men and their words and actions, which variously move us to laughter, suspense, and even—in the case of the ancient leaders—to compassion. In meeting a responsibility which he shares with the narrative writer, Shakespeare has created a scene which we value not merely as a means by which the story is begun but for the vigorous emotional satisfactions which it conveys.

Having noted one or two rather particular specimens of the way in which Brooke's narrative is presented by the dramatist, we may find it worthwhile to glance very briefly at some of the more general ways in which we sense that the tale has been altered in Shakespeare's treatment. Even in our discussion of the first scene, we found ourself describing Shakespeare's achievement as that of finding suitable means for gaining essentially the same ends as does the corresponding passage in Brooke's poem. But in *Romeo and Juliet,* as in most notable dramatic treatments of narrative materials, there are fundamental changes which must be seen as far more than necessary steps in "dramatization." They must be viewed, rather, as affirmative responses to the special opportunities afforded by the drama for unique literary creation. Accordingly, no great play, whatever its narrative source, is a mere "adaptation," for the drama is not merely one of several alternative modes of communication for the storyteller. It is, on the contrary, a vigorously independent literary kind, affording its own rich opportunities for the achievement of its own unmistakable effects. And the true dramatist does not scruple, whatever the source of his materials, to shape and alter them in any aspect in order to exploit to the fullest the advantages presented by the general character of dramatic art.

Among the most interesting changes which Shakespeare has made in the story, we should note that the action, represented by Brooke as occurring over a period of nine months, is compressed to a span of six days. Shakespeare accomplishes this not only by beginning his tale at a point far along in Romeo's infatuated love affair with Rosaline and immediately before the Capulet feast but by creating of the wedding night, which precedes several weeks of married bliss in Brooke, a crowded series of crucial events. Among other very basic changes is the introduction of Mercutio as a thoroughly developed character whose death prompts Romeo's slaying of Tybalt as an understandable act of vengeance rather than an accidental consequence of a street brawl. The nurse, too, appears for the first time in Shakespeare's play in her full comic dimension, serving as well as an indispensable element in the advancement of the plot. In addition, Shakespeare departs from Brooke in other less explicit but equally significant ways which various kinds of close scrutiny, including statistical analysis, might make entirely clear. The speeches in Brooke's poem—and it does contain a number of them—are, for example, much longer on the average than those in the play. Shakespeare's characterization is far more thorough and hence more sharply contrasting than that of Brooke; we can discern, that is, much more in the speeches of Shakespeare's characters which invites us to assign to them their highly individual habits, values, and patterns of thought. Perhaps most striking, although least tangible, is the tempo or "pace" by which Shakespeare's dramatic dialogue, for all its lyrical flights, comic interludes, and intellectual reflections, awakens and sustains within us a sense of spectatorship, a feeling that we are eyewitnesses to the uninterrupted enactment of a single, absorbing sequence of events.

None of these notable aspects of Shakespeare's play can be regarded merely as his solution to a specific problem raised by the conversion of the traditional story into dramatic form. They are not, that is, mere changes which Shakespeare made to conform to the requirements of the dramatic manner. Rather they represent his affirmative exploitation of the great general resources of the drama as a literary form. Shakespeare's compression of time was not necessary in order that a play be made of Brooke's poem, but it is a compression invited by the dramatic manner—and *Romeo and Juliet* is a better play because of it. As, in the following pages, we discuss certain general facts about the drama, the reader should sense that the ultimate success of a playwright like Shakespeare lies not only in his solution of the problems with which his art confronts him but in the way in which he seizes upon its opportunities.

To appreciate the distinguishing features of the dramatist's art, however, we are bound to remind ourselves of some of the limitations which the dramatic form traditionally imposes upon an author. Of these the most conspicuous arises, as we have already noted in our discussion of *Romeo and Juliet*, from the playwright's inability directly to address his audience. Some devices—such as spoken prologues, epilogues, and, most importantly, the choruses which originated in the Greek theater—permit the playwright a certain amount of direct comment and exposition. And there are dramatists, like George Bernard Shaw, who, apparently assuming their works will be widely read, include, in the printed version, lengthy prefaces, stage directions, and other auxiliary materials. Yet the play proper—as it unfolds a fictional action upon the stage—offers little opportunity for the dramatist to speak in his own person. From this fact it follows that for many ends which are achieved by direct exposition in narrative fiction the playwright must depend exclusively upon the words his characters speak. Thus the narration of events which do not actually occur upon the stage, the establishment of character in its many aspects, whatever features of setting and environment are not literally discernible as dramatic spectacles, and, perhaps most important, all of the "internal" action—the states of mind, thoughts, emotions, decisions, and other unexpressed experiences which the novelist is free to describe as he chooses—must emerge entirely in whatever can be heard and seen by the audience.

And the audience for the drama is a very different creature from the anonymous, invisible reader to whom the narrative work is addressed. It has been gathered, from many different places, upon the promise of entertainment, to form a temporarily united, very tangible group, willing to devote at the most a few hours to a single exposure to a work of art. For most playwrights, the nature of this audience poses formidable problems. The drama is not ordinarily created in order to be studied by reflective persons at convenient moments. The playwright can take few chances that his meaning will be obscure or subject to misunderstanding. He must have some assurance that important facts will be noted and remembered by his audience—for the playgoer cannot turn back to earlier pages to refresh his memory. To speak, therefore, of the playwright's sense of "showmanship" is not to debase his art in any way; it is merely to recognize that the theatrical audience of virtually any time or society is brought together under certain clear and special circumstances and therefore imposes clear and special conditions upon the playwright. For, in effect, the audience seeks from the play a single experience which can be grasped and understood in its entirety and which can be seen, when the final curtain falls, as essentially unambiguous, complete, and memorable.

Other challenges uniquely confront the dramatist. In one sense, for example, performance by living actors lends immediacy and credibility to this kind of literature. On the other hand, the illusion of reality which the theater conveys is a precarious business, and, when it is threatened, the success of the entire play is threatened as well. Theatrical audiences are prepared to suspend their ordinary skepticism about many things. They are willing to believe the playwright's assertion that the stage is whatever place he chooses it to be; they cheerfully forget that actors have any identity other than the fictional one they have assumed; they are willing, rather miraculously, to assume the role of spectators of events in real life and, to a degree rarely attained in the reading of fiction, to respond unabashedly to the drama with emotions which only reality itself can ordinarily elicit. But precisely because the playgoer goes this far in his willingness to believe, he is particularly resentful of excessive demands upon his credulity. He has made, that is, certain concessions in the expectation of finding upon the stage that which is convincing and hence agreeably moving; if, in its violation of basic principles of probability, what he sees is not credible, he will be the more disappointed. Thus he expects that events will reflect some sort of intelligible relationship, that in their motives and their actions the characters will display, at the least, a consistency which is reasonable and satisfying.

This does not mean, of course, that the mundane, common-sense notions of what is physically probable or even possible must prevail in the world of the theater. The playwright is at liberty to construct his own universe of almost complete fantasy. Within even such a universe, however, the audience expects a certain plausibility and order. The playwright sets his own rules as to what is relevant and probable and, although we generally accept the rules without question, we assume that, by the most elementary principles of logic, they will be observed throughout the play. Thus, for example, in the world of *Romeo and Juliet* we are prepared for and cheerfully accept the workings of accident, coincidence, and abrupt, inexplicable passion. But Shakespeare has also established certain patterns of behavior for his characters and, indeed, a prevailing climate for the world which surrounds them; in the tight economy of the drama, deviations from these established standards would be difficult to explain away. In Shakespeare's fictional Verona, the singular circumstances of the lovers' deaths seem plausible enough; but a cowardly act by Romeo —or an unchaste one by Juliet—would violently jar our sense of what is credible.

Finally, it is rather obvious that the physical characteristics of the stage impose distinct limitations upon the playwright. Some of these, while they appear trivial, can only be solved in ways which clearly affect the play, even in its printed version. There are many passages in dramatic works which can be explained satisfactorily only if we understand the demands—some of them quite commonplace—with which the physical nature of the stage confronts the dramatist. A famous example is the ending of *Hamlet*, in which, to a funeral march, the dead bodies are solemnly borne away, not so much as a piece of concluding ritual as a means for removing the corpses from a stage which, in Shakespeare's time, had no curtain. And in *Romeo and Juliet*, the choice of such settings as Juliet's chamber, the balcony, the friar's cell, and the tomb is clearly dictated by particular features of the Elizabethan stage.[1]

Where conventional modes of dramatic production are employed, shiftings of place which are numerous and rapid are clearly impractical—and, in addition to the mechanical difficulties involved, place an additional burden upon the credulity and patience of the audience. Even in the motion pictures and television, for that matter, the mobility of the camera is not unlimited, and the story is generally developed through a series of distinct scenes which, while usually greater in number

[1] For an illuminating analysis of the stage directions in *Romeo and Juliet* and the degree to which the physical features of the stage dictate the choice of scene, the student should consult *Shakespeare: The Major Plays and the Sonnets*, ed. G. B. Harrison (New York: Harcourt, Brace & Co., 1949), pp. 56–58.

than those of the legitimate theater, still impose upon the script-writer restrictions which he shares with the theatrical playwright and from which the novelist is free.

Dramatists, of course, enjoy great latitude in the uses which they may make of the stage. As we are all aware, certain plays call for stagings which, as sources of both verisimilitude and aesthetic satisfaction, seem indispensable to the total effect of the work. At the opposite extreme are plays which rely upon the merest suggestion, if any, of the setting in which the action occurs. But, whatever the playwright chooses to make of his stage, he, once again, sets rules by which we expect him to abide; when, for example, he indicates that his performance will rely heavily on a full complement of scenery and physical "properties" to convey the illusion of reality, we anticipate that his effect will be sustained by consistent adherence to these devices. In short, the stage is a tool which affords vast and flexible resources yet has its clear limitations, and from the playwright's employment of it we expect taste, relevance, and consistency.

In suggesting some limitations upon the dramatist's art, we have, in one sense, been listing handicaps which the playwright, as contrasted to the narrative writer, must face and overcome. But it would be a great mistake to assume that these facts about the theater and its audience are entirely negative forces which must be borne in mind by a tolerant reader. On the contrary, many of the most impressive qualities of successful drama are present, as we have already suggested, precisely because the playwright finds it necessary to carry out his task with a rigor and ingenuity which are not demanded in equal degree of the novelist.

As a rule, the *plot* of a dramatic work emerges with great clarity. The theatrical audience does not browse or deliberate but concentrates its attention upon an action and its outcome. To be sure, the literature of the theater contains works which are above all discursive or in which shapeless, disjointed, or inconclusive plots apparently subserve some end other than the representation of a unified human action. For the most part, however, dramatic works allow us to perceive more plainly than do most novels the actual structure of the plot. As we have already said, the economy of time and means within which the dramatist works imposes upon him a fairly austere principle of relevance and any substantial portion of his play can usually be accounted for by its contribution to a central action.

The qualities of plot which we have noted in narrative fiction—the conflicts and their resolutions, the reversals and discoveries—are present in the drama as well and, in this medium, are ordinarily easier to discern than in works of prose fiction. Since the dramatist is limited to the representation of overt statements and acts, we are frequently aware of the precise moments of significant change—of recognition, decision, success, failure, and the heights and depths of response which they elicit from the characters.

Perhaps this awareness accounts for our willingness to identify, with certain conventional terms, the parts of a dramatic plot, for although we can often discern the analogues of such parts in the plots of novels and short stories, this identification seems less illuminating when applied to narrative prose.

Thus, in a play, the relevant circumstances which exist at the start of a dramatic action are made clear through what is often called the _exposition_. The exposition may be regarded as antecedent to the plot itself; it reveals, that is, a state of affairs from which the plot proceeds. (Used in this sense, the term must be distinguished from—although it is plainly related to—

its more general application to the means employed, at any point in the play, for describing facts and occurrences which are not presented before the audience.) The circumstances which emerge in the exposition may be, as it were, "constant," involving, that is, no fact which makes a change inevitable. In such instances it is a change, actual or threatened, in the status quo which may be said to mark the beginning of the plot proper. In *Romeo and Juliet*, we must know of the hostility between the Capulets and Montagues, but however fraught with potential trouble this initial situation may be, it is not until Romeo and Juliet fall in love that there emerges a specific "problem" which demands resolution and which precipitates the course of action which constitutes the plot. Similar expositions, revealing situations which, while tense and uneasy, contain no facts which make future change and action inevitable, are to be found in *Hamlet* and *Othello*. In other plays, however, the exposition may reveal a state of affairs which patently includes the genesis of the action—a question which directly calls for an answer, a condition which must without doubt have significant consequences. Sophocles' great tragedy, *Oedipus the King*, is such a play, for at the very beginning of the drama we learn from the suppliant citizens of Thebes that a plague has fallen upon their city and that their king, Oedipus, must seek to banish the affliction by an inquiry which, as it turns out, leads to his terrible discovery and tragic fall. In such a work, the exposition virtually coincides with the beginning of the central action and therefore, as an independent, quantitative part of the dramatic structure, can claim very little importance.

Following the exposition it is possible, in the majority of plays, to trace the development of plot from its inception through what is often called the *complication*. As its name implies, complication is that stage of the drama in which the plot acquires increasing complexity, issues are likely to multiply and intensify, and the suspense and emotional engagement of the audience presumably become greater. In most plays in which it is possible to speak of a complication, this portion of the plot is, quantitatively, the largest. For it seems to be inherent in the dramatist's method (and, indeed, in the broad meaning of the term "dramatic") that major emphasis be placed upon "build-up," upon, that is, the magnifying, multiplying, and cumulative intensifying of challenges and dilemmas and of the suspense which they engender.

We are all familiar with the word *climax*, and when we are seeing or reading a play our natural sense of what is "climactic" will generally reveal to us the emotional "high point" in our experience with the work. Ordinarily, this point will coincide with the structural climax of the play, if we define this stage as the ultimate one in the complication—that state of greatest complexity, in which the issues appear at their most acute and call most urgently for resolution. The climax, as a rule, embodies an encounter, a discovery, a decision, or some similar occurrence which tends to resolve the questions and tensions which have been developed systematically through the complication. In the conspicuously climactic moments of the theater, the dramatist strives to incorporate much that is inherently exciting, and these moments take such forms as open confrontation, direct physical combat, critical decision, and critical discovery. The power of the climax, however, vitally depends on what has preceded it and on our recognition that the climactic action will largely determine the outcome of the principal issues in which the play has engaged us.

Where the parts of a dramatic plot are sufficiently discernible to be identified by technical terms, the climax is usually succeeded—or often accompanied—by an "unraveling" of whatever has been vexed and tangled in the affairs of the characters. What has been bewildering is explained; what has been disorderly or uncertain is restored to a state of repose— whether this is the original or a new one. The questions and conflicts about which the dramatic action has centered are resolved, happily or unhappily, and the audience, however it may choose to reflect upon what it has seen, is no longer compelled to ask "what happens next." This final stage of plot is referred to as the _dénouement._ It may be a very brisk affair, at least partially coinciding with the climax (for example, in a play where a single critical conflict or choice determines decisively the conclusion of principal lines of action). On the other hand, the dénouement may be a relatively protracted series of occurrences which, although they follow the climax and do not share its intensity, are required to reveal how, in Puck's words,

> Jack shall have Jill;
> Nought shall go ill;
> The man shall have his mare again, and all shall be well.

The choice of the dramatic manner by an author not only tends to affect the structure of his plot but, even more clearly, governs the method and the order by which its incidents and their attendant circumstances are presented. The playwright's inability to address his audience directly, for example, can lead to his adoption of certain recognized techniques for the indirect representation of action and exposition. _Narration_ itself is almost indispensable to the dramatist, for it is an exceptional play in which all incidents necessary for the understanding of the plot are viewed as current activities upon the stage. Many factors, including artistic economy and the physical character of the theater, compel the employment of _narrative speeches_ in which events and situations are recounted by characters. In the Greek theater, indeed, it was customary to avoid the performance of acts of physical violence upon the stage and, instead, such episodes were reported through "messenger speeches," in which critical occurrences were described by eyewitnesses of various kinds.

In *Romeo and Juliet,* narration, while neither very frequent nor sustained, is employed at points where it seems expedient. The crucial episode, for example, in which Friar John, charged with conveying to Romeo the true facts concerning Friar Laurence's scheme, is detained in the house of sickness, is directly narrated in its proper place by Brooke. (Interestingly enough, the popular motion picture version of the play also depicts this incident, although without dialogue.) Shakespeare, however, has chosen—perhaps for reasons of economy, perhaps because the episode interrupts our pursuit of the lovers' fate, or perhaps because it affords so little opportunity for dialogue—to inform us of this occurrence through the report of the frustrated monk on his return to Friar Laurence's cell.

In the theater of our own day, narration, while less formally and hence somewhat more naturally introduced than in the Greek messenger speeches, continues to play an important part in the presentation of the plot. Incidents both antecedent and intrinsic to the central action become known, that is, through accounts provided by the characters and, while they function significantly in the context of the drama, such speeches often display much the same power as traditional narrative prose or poetry.

In his *characterization,* the dramatist is encouraged, by the very limitations we have been considering, to achieve a kind of clarity and strength which is sometimes missing in narrative forms. Within the economy in which he works, the playwright cannot always represent his characters in the fully developed, many-faceted way which is available to the novelist, but for precisely this reason those aspects of character which have genuine relevance for the drama are persistently and artfully stressed. As careful psychological descriptions, the characterizations in *Romeo and Juliet* are patently fragmentary and superficial; we know little of Romeo save his gallantry and passion, of Juliet save her innocence and fidelity, of the Nurse save her bawdiness and devotion. Yet these are qualities which we do not doubt and cannot forget. Because a playwright is, moreover, barred from the abstractions and generalizations which the novelist may employ, he tends to rely heavily on what we have already described as the major index of character in any literary work—namely the *choices* made by characters in specific situations. While it is true that there are other devices for conveying traits of character (the opinions of one character concerning another, for example, or the various aspects of physical appearance which can color our views), what the individual character says and does—the course of action he selects when the choice is significant—serves, above all else, to form the judgments of the audience. To put it simply, we know the characters in a play not from what the author tells us but from direct observation.

In the conveyance of *thought*, the playwright is again limited to the speeches of his characters. There are, to be sure, devices by which the internal intellectual activities of the drama are presented. Among these are the *soliloquy* and the so-called *aside* (in which, by a change of voice, the actor expresses himself for the benefit of the audience but not for the other characters upon the stage). Although a play like *Romeo and Juliet* abounds in these devices, the major source of our inferences concerning the thoughts of dramatic characters, particularly in the modern theater, is almost always authentic dialogue—actual conversation. Many plays can be regarded as highly intellectual works, and there are dramas by men like Shaw and Ibsen which seem to invite our attention primarily because they formulate and attack problems of interest and urgency and provide attitudes and conclusions which we assign implicitly to the playwright himself. But even if we go so far, when confronted by such a work, as to suspend our interest in its imaginative qualities and view it as we might a philosophic dialogue, we remain in the presence of a dramatic *fiction*, and whatever qualities of thought we assign to the author follow entirely from the ideas which his imaginary characters have expressed in our presence.

In dealing with *setting*, the playwright faces additional special problems. He is, to be sure, at liberty to draw upon various material resources of the stage in establishing the immediate physical environment for his action. The reader of a play should note, therefore, the use which the dramatist makes of scenery, costumes, furniture, and "properties"—the last, a term which designates the essentially portable articles which lend conviction to the performance but can, like the handkerchief in *Othello*, serve as a focus of attention and become uniquely dramatic. For setting in its broader sense—for the conveying of general qualities of time, place, and atmosphere which the novelist is free to describe with great elaboration—the dramatist remains largely dependent upon representative particulars. The tangible resources of the theater may be helpful, for settings, costumes, and properties can eloquently suggest, for example, the flavor of a particular society or period. The less tangible aspects of a given environment, however, including prevailing habits, values, and institutions, must emerge in dialogue and action. What we might call "collective characterization"—the strident, savage, and unsympathetic society of Verona, for example, which so directly affects the fate of Romeo and Juliet—can become understood only as it is manifested in the particular, if representative, words and deeds of individuals.

We have thus far been discussing ways in which, by comparison with the narrative writer, the dramatist appears to some extent limited in his use of the elements of literary art. It is worth repeating that, even when seen in this light, the art of the dramatist ought not to be regarded as one which seeks merely to overcome handicaps and adjust to special situations; for precisely because the drama, in some respects, is restricted, it often achieves, particularly in dialogue, a unique clarity, vigor, and attractiveness. At this point, however, we must recognize that drama also enjoys its peculiar *advantages* over narrative fiction and particularly that the playwright, while he may face certain limitations, has at his command one special and very valuable source of help. This source is the audience itself. For the audience in the theater—and the thoughtful reader of plays should strive in some measure to become a member of the audience—is prepared to make concessions to the playwright which are granted to no other kind of literary artist. These concessions, in the main, are represented by what we call *conventions*. They reflect a sort of common agreement, by the audiences of a particular society, as to what should be expected from the dramatist. Some conventions arise from a general acceptance of the obvious restrictions which the nature of the dramatic medium imposes upon the playwright. Others develop from the needs and demands of the audience itself—from a realistic assessment of the patience and perceptiveness of which a theatrical audience is capable. Still other conventions develop historically as consequences of various forces—economic, religious, social, and so forth—which affect the theater as a cultural institution.

The effect of convention is likely to strike the modern reader most forcibly when it is encountered in the drama of a society other than our own. Thus the presence of the chorus in Greek drama may seem alien and distracting until we accept it as a traditional component in the plays of that period. Seen in this light, the chorus is of unusual interest, since it often represents, among other things, an effort at direct communication between playwright and audience. Similarly, by recognizing that the Elizabethan stage employed only male actors, we are able to attribute to this convention certain qualities of Shakespeare's characters and to understand the original theatrical impact of such situations as the impersonation of males by female characters within his plots.

Convention, however, is as indispensable to the theater of today as to that of any previous period. Perhaps the most obvious and fundamental of all conventions is that which prompts our implicit acceptance of the role of eavesdropper and eyewitness and enables us to find in the proscenium opening of the stage—whether as a nonexistent fourth wall to a room or a hypothetical expanse of space—a sort of magic window into a fictional world. In accepting this basic role we are, as it were, implicitly agreeing to countless other conventions and assenting, in effect, to the playwright's use of a series of traditional devices as "signals" to indicate such things as the passing of time, the shifting of place, and the many other things which cannot literally occur within the theater. We are willing, as well, to accept changing conventions which invite us to enter into new agreements with the dramatist, as technical or artistic developments seem to require them. Thus in recent years, "theater in the round," in some ways a throwback to earlier modes of dramatic production, has prompted us to accept as a new convention a stage from which the familiar directions and proportions have largely disappeared. And in the newer media of communication—motion picture, radio, and television—which make possible the presentation of dramatic works under totally novel conditions, we have adjusted, with various degrees of enthusiasm, to conventions dictated not only by inescapable physical facts but by economic and rhetorical considerations as well.

Convention cannot be seen merely as a set of customs which surround and condition the experience of theater-going. Convention is capable of affecting, in the most fundamental ways, the actual shape and character of the dramatic work. The division of plays into acts and scenes is, in the broad sense of the term, conventional. Its origin doubtless lies partially in the playwright's practical need to indicate changes in the location of his action as well as to suggest the passage of time. Possibly it lies, as well, in an equally practical awareness that the patience and powers of concentration of any audience have their limits. Whatever the reason, there persists in the history of the theater a tendency to impose upon the drama some kind of meaningful division into quantitative parts—although the precise character and significance of these divisions varies widely through the years. Even within the history of the European theater, the definition and importance both of acts and of scenes change conspicuously. In the stagecraft of an earlier period, for example, the playwright could, with little if any alteration of his simple physical set, arbitrarily indicate changes in the location of his action and, in consequence, individual scenes within acts were more varied and numerous than they are today.

As a principal unit of dramatic organization, the scene deserves considerable attention, both in its individual structure and in its relationship to the entire play. A scene of any appreciable length calls for its own autonomous principles of development, which are often analogous to those which embrace the total dramatic work. Important scenes generally contain a "climax" and an artful interplay of relaxation and tension. The animation, variety, and "pace" which we associate with successful drama are dependent fundamentally on the playwright's ability to sustain these qualities in each of the separate scenes. However moving the total plot may be, a single tedious or distracting scene is capable of "bogging down" the drama in a way from which it may never recover.

Relationship and balance between scenes is likewise a matter of great importance. The habits of theatrical audiences (quite as much as any abstract standard of proportion) call for a certain orderly diversity of scene. Emotional tension cannot be unduly protracted; the effects of any single kind of dramatic situation diminish with repetition; attention wavers unless challenged with novelty. Thus the scenes of a play tend to be balanced and contrasted with one another in terms of such variables as length, intensity, seriousness, and, obviously, setting and participating characters. Often we find scenes, indeed, which deliberately suspend our engagement in the principal course of action in order to introduce what is referred to as "relief." From the standpoint of purely literary analysis, it is sometimes difficult to justify the introduction of scenes which do not directly advance or illuminate the plot; certain of the famous comic scenes injected into Shakespeare's greatest tragedies raise such analytic problems. But from the standpoint of "showmanship," in which the attention and sympathy of a living audience are paramount, it is not difficult to understand the function of these brisk and, in themselves, highly artful opportunities for "respite" from the compelling demands of serious drama.

In the modern theater, the formal designation of scenes, signaled by the lowering of the curtain, is increasingly infrequent. Yet we continue to think of plays as a series of "scenes," if only because we use the term to refer to single, more or less complete episodes and conversations. Acts, on the other hand, still tend to represent major divisions of the work, often set apart by the passage of time, and, more importantly, representative of distinct and basic stages in the development of the plot. Even the act, however, is not an indispensable convention in the modern theater, and there are contemporary playwrights who, while they concede the audience an intermission or two, do not acknowledge that the dramatic action is divisable in any significant way. It is interesting, as well, to note that traditional notions of scene and act disappear or are redefined when dramatic works appear through such new media as motion pictures or television. In the movies, these divisions rarely occur, while broadcast drama is presently shaped, for better or for worse, by such economically engendered conventions as the commercial announcement, the "station-break," and the sacred, if inexplicable, taboo against program units of other than fifteen, thirty, or sixty minutes' duration.

In many other ways, the structure and content of plays can be directly affected by theatrical convention. We have already spoken of the soliloquy and the "aside" as devices by which the internal thoughts and feelings of characters can be communicated to an audience. While these conventions appear somewhat cumbersome and archaic today, in some instances they have been succeeded by experiments which seek substantially the same end. Thus, in some of Eugene O'Neill's plays, the characters step aside to deliver lines which are frankly distinguished from ordinary dialogue as representing unspoken thoughts, while, in certain motion pictures, the sound track is used independently of the picture to much the same effect.

Similarly the prologues, epilogues, and choruses which, in the theater of other times, have represented attempts by the playwright directly to address his audience have been succeeded, in certain modern plays, by "stage managers," narrators, and similar spokesmen for the author. And the traditional function of the "messenger speech," itself a well-defined convention of the Greek drama, is today being carried out in characteristically modern ways, ranging from procedures which, like the motion picture "flashback," basically affect the structure of the work to such simple but ingenious devices as the narrative summary provided by a radio broadcast within the play.

Although our discussion of the relationship between literary works and the historic circumstances of their composition is reserved for our final chapter, it must be noted here that dramatic conventions in any period reflect far more than the rules and customs of the theater alone. Much as we admire the magnificent love passages in *Romeo and Juliet*, for example, their unabashed lyricism, rich imagery, and extravagant passion would probably appear forced and "unreal" in a modern play. These qualities themselves, quite apart from the level to which they are elevated by Shakespeare's genius, are the products of general conventions which governed the character of most love-literature, whether in prose, verse, or drama, in Shakespeare's day. Not only qualities of diction but the recurrence of certain kinds of incident can be seen as the conventional manifestation of certain prevailing customs and beliefs. The *deus ex machina*, a term now generally applied to unexpected, decisive interventions in the action of any story, was originally a Greek theatrical device, involving the descent of a deity, by means of a mechanical contrivance, for the purpose of resolving the difficulties encountered by the human characters of the drama. Yet the presence of this purely theatrical phenomenon was made acceptable to the audience primarily because—as we can see in a work like the *Iliad*—the general climate of taste and belief lent credibility and interest to the notion of divine intervention in human affairs. And, doubtless, there is much in the drama of our own day, whether it reaches us in the theater or through the movies or broadcasting, which would have seemed incredible or disagreeable to the audiences of a former time but which the conventions of literature and the values of contemporary society render acceptable to the modern audience.

Convention then can be seen not only as a bulwark in the dramatist's practice of his art but as a major force in shaping the finished dramatic work. Beyond this, the playwright has at his disposal other obvious resources which, while they are only indirectly related to the actual construction of the drama, should be kept in mind by any reader who wishes to sense the total effect of the work as it appears on the stage. In principle, the playwright can anticipate that the qualities of the human voice and appearance, ingenuity of direction, beauty and aptness of setting, and the whole amalgam of spectacle, movement, and sound which contributes so vitally to the illusion of the theater will bring into being, in its final form, the concrete image of the play he has written.

Thus, although the prospect of ultimate performance imposes its limitations upon the dramatist, as we have said, it also allows him to share his task with other persons of diversified talents. As a literary artist, the playwright is relieved of certain tasks which ordinarily confront the narrative writer. His mission as an author is complete with the "reading version" of the play and, whatever he may contribute to the subsequent "acting version," with its detailed directions for stage presentation, is the product of other than literary arts. In most printed plays, for example, we find physical actions described very briefly. And, in his characterization, however profound and complicated it may be, the playwright tends, unlike the narrative writer, to be circumspect in his prescriptions concerning the appearance and mannerisms of his characters. These are clearly matters which the director and performers must "work out" with their own special skills. There are, indeed, in many plays some rather fundamental ambiguities which, deliberate or not, can be resolved only by decisions regarding actual performance. Those students who have seen more than one actor in the role of *Hamlet*, for example, should be aware how even so great and "literary" a play depends for its precise effect upon the interpretation which an individual actor places upon the character of its hero.

It is this distinction between the literary artistry required in the writing of a play and the other, equally admirable talents required for its actual performance which should prove encouraging to the student—who is more often likely to read plays than to attend them. As we have pointed out, the dramatist is a literary artist to the extent—and it is inevitably a very great extent—that he achieves his effect through the representation, in language, of human activity. The structure and quality of the language, more often than not, are affected by the prospect of ultimate theatrical production, and therefore it is obviously valuable to read plays in an awareness of the way in which their dramatic manner shapes their literary character. Yet, by a recognition of the special qualities of the playwright's art, we should be led finally to an increased appreciation of the fundamental union which exists among all imaginative artists who employ the powers of language in the moving representation of human affairs.

4

THE POEM AS HISTORIC FACT

In the chapter called "Reading Lyric Poems," a poem was defined as "the product of deliberate, artful construction in language, designed to stand in permanent form, with the capacity to bring pleasure to those who hear or read it." This definition suggested that our concern should center consistently upon the poetic work itself, that the questions we ask should be directed fundamentally to increasing our own pleasure in encounters with particular products of literary art.

When we employed this approach in the examination of three poems, we were concerned with questions which, with few exceptions, could be answered by an inspection of the poems themselves. We attempted to isolate and describe various elements in poetry and to recognize the many ways in which, singly and in relationship to each other, they can account for the effects which are achieved by individual poems. We avoided deliberately many questions of a historical character: biographical facts about the poet, speculations about the circumstances under which the poem was written, inquiries into the many factors which could have influenced the substance and the language chosen by a particular poet at a particular time. Our assumption was that the pleasure to be derived uniquely from poetry is provided by the poem itself—that a lyric by Keats or a tragedy by Shakespeare is an aesthetic experience for us only as it lies before us in the here and now, as it affects our living, twentieth-century selves.

At the same time, however, we cannot deny that any work of art is, in a literal sense, a historic fact. It was created by an artist who, whether or not we know much about him, lived and wrote at a specific time and under specific circumstances which inevitably account for some of the qualities of his art. Very often a poem itself will tell us all we need to know about the motives of its creator; communication, and its emotional and intellectual consequences for the reader, proceed in the way which was presumably intended by the poet. But because the writing of a poem is a historic fact and because history involves change, it is obvious that what may have been clear to the original readers of a poem sometimes will not be entirely clear to us. In such instances we are interested in achieving contact with the audience for whom the poem was intended— in understanding the particular beliefs, values, habits, and knowledge which the poet assumed would be brought to bear upon his work. Sometimes the acquisition of such understanding is an effortless matter, requiring only that we draw upon the knowledge ordinarily shared by educated people. The *Iliad*, for example, can be enthusiastically appreciated without any profound investigation into the history of Greek civilization, because the average thoughtful reader comes to this epic poem equipped to understand that it is the product of religious beliefs different from his own, to respond sympathetically to moral values that seem somewhat distorted in our own day, to sense that the struggle which is being described is related to the historic roots of a great civilization. On the other hand, although we have little difficulty in sympathizing with Hamlet, or in grasping the essential character of his dilemma, our full understanding of Shakespeare's play depends upon our possession of at least one special fact, namely that in Shakespeare's time the marriage between Gertrude and her brother-in-law would have been regarded as incestuous. And it is easy to think of other, far more important historic changes which impede communication between an author of the past and his present-day audience. Of these, changes in the character of language provide the most obvious example; the barrier between Chaucer and the modern reader can be overcome only when we exploit the products of specialized linguistic research.

It is important to be aware of the way in which historic meaning often must be recovered in order to provide a satisfactory response to a literary work of the past. Any student of literature should recognize the debt he owes to the researches of historians, editors, and linguists, and he should recognize, too, that his reading will make demands upon his own historical knowledge or his ability to acquire it. But this closing of the gaps produced by temporal and cultural distance is only one way in which the "external" factors surrounding literary composition are important. For there is a more affirmative, if more subtle, way in which our response to a poem can be enriched by the recognition that it is the product of an individual artist who is susceptible to many general and special influences in his historic environment.

A poem is what the poet chooses to make it. Yet his choice is conditioned inevitably by influences to which, in common with at least some other men, he is exposed throughout his life. Even if he deliberately chooses to reject those influences, the rejection itself often becomes conspicuous. Indeed, the full measure of the poet's individuality, and hence of his achievement, becomes apparent only when we set in balance those qualities of his writing which he shares with others and those which are the unique reflection of his individual talent.

The attempt to identify and describe significant qualities which several poets or poems seem to share and which can be traced to common influences has led scholars to employ many kinds of *classification*. Poets have been grouped together on the basis of a common historical period, a common influential teacher or predecessor. Such superficial classifications, however, usually serve only as general labels which imply that there are significant qualities which the works of men thus categorized have in common. To speak of a "Victorian" poem or novel or building is ordinarily to do more than locate its genesis in a particular historical period; it is to suggest that the work possesses certain features which are generally recognized as marking the products of that period. And to speak, as has recently been done, of certain young poets of the "San Francisco school" is not merely to note their common geographical location but to observe that the work of all the poets so designated presents strong common characteristics—that "San Francisco," in this context, stands for a certain *kind* of verse.

Moreover, many influences which writers share have very little directly to do with time or place. Ideas have a stalwart, independent history of their own, and beliefs, enthusiasms, and problems have a wonderful capacity to communicate themselves through periods of time and across stretches of space. Thus it is possible to speak of "tendencies" and "traditions" which, transcending the limits of a particular place or period, emerge in widely diversified works which are still linked by common qualities. Terms like "classicism" and "romanticism" are controversial and perhaps not very productive, but the frequency with which they have been employed suggests at the very least a *sense* of two kinds of art which can be roughly defined and distinguished from each other in the huge miscellany of works produced by the artists of recent centuries.

We have spoken of "common influences" to which writers are exposed without, as yet, considering what such influences are likely to be or how they operate. Many of them are obvious. First of all, it is apparent that the poet as a man—or woman —responds in many respects to precisely the same influences as his non-poet contemporaries, that he is affected by the wisdom, the attitudes, the occurrences, and the issues of the world about him. It is equally clear that—perhaps somewhat more than the ordinary man—the poet will have an awareness of the great cumulative body of ideas and facts which can be described as his general intellectual tradition. Unlike many other kinds of "specialists," the poet does not find an area which is circumscribed for his professional attention; if the world of the past—or of the future—concerns him more than does the here and now, he is no less a poet for this. Finally, the poet is likely to be influenced by other poets—his predecessors as well as his contemporaries. He is likely to join with some of them in a concern for the same problems, an interest in the same techniques; he is at liberty to imitate them, to attempt to improve upon them, or, quite possibly, deliberately to reject them in principle or in practice.

Beyond such observations as we have made so far it is difficult to go on generalizing upon the influences which affect the creation of a literary work. Where we feel justified in describing an artistic "period" or "tendency" or "tradition," we do so because the qualities which we feel are common to the group so described also serve to distinguish the group and to establish for it a significant identity in the history of art. The validity and usefulness of such categories is of obvious concern to the historian of books and ideas. And the researches and interpretations of scholarly specialists are often fascinating to the reader, who has every reason to be interested in whatever responsible generalizations can be derived from any body of works with which he is familiar.

As ordinary readers, however, rather than as critics or historians, we are chiefly interested in the power of such classifications to illuminate the work of art as it immediately confronts us. What is required of us is an awareness of relevant historical fact rather than disciplined skill in the process of historical recovery. Our principal responsibility is to preserve a sort of broad-mindedness which can reconcile us to what, at first sight, may seem alien or inexplicable in the literary practices we encounter. We must, that is, understand that many of the artistic choices revealed by any literary work may be the reflection of habits, preoccupations, and opinion which can be explained only by the artist's temporal identity.

Somewhat paradoxically, we often find it harder to accept this responsibility when we are confronted with the art of our own time than when we are considering the products of the past. In the latter situation, it would seem, we are cheerfully prepared to exploit the work of the historian and, with his help, to enter into the spirit of audiences very different from those of our own age. In part, perhaps, because we have no such comfortable generalizations to guide us, we seem much less certain in our response to whatever is novel about the writing—or painting or music—of our contemporaries. But here too the impediments to our appreciation may yield to an awareness of time and place, of society and its ideas, and of the current of literary history which, assuredly, has not ceased to flow upon its entry into our own era.

In the rest of this chapter we shall be discussing chiefly the body of writing which is commonly referred to as "modern poetry." Narrowly speaking, our approach is not "historical," if by this term we mean that we are considering facts which belong exclusively to the past. But to read imaginative literature with historical awareness is to apply relevant facts and generalizations, whatever their source and whatever historic period they involve, to our own experience with a specific work. In the case of any of the modern arts we need not rely centrally upon the reconstructions and schemes which others have prepared for us. In large measure we share the circumstances under which contemporary literature is produced, and the "history" which shapes the writing of our time is found in the life and the art which immediately surround us.

In one sense, the term "modern" is a chronological classification which can be applied, legitimately enough, to the writing of any poet of the present or recent past. Yet the term "modern" at least implicitly refers to a certain general *kind* of writing which is found in much of the poetry of this period. In consequence, critics and editors are not reluctant to label as "modern" the works of such people as Gerard Manley Hopkins or Emily Dickinson, although both of these poets died in the 1880's, while, on the other hand, certain poets still living have shown little interest in contemporary poetic practices and, as "traditional" writers, can be quite clearly distinguished from the representatives of modern writing. It is most important to note, moreover, that while there are certain qualities which we can *generally* discern in modern poetry there is no one of them about which we can say more than that it is *likely* to appear in a modern poem. In fact, although we shall discuss certain features of modern poetry in some detail, the student must be aware that he will probably never find a single poem in which all of these features appear any more than he will be able to discover any single quality which is the inevitable hallmark of a modern poem.

The characteristics of modern poetry are not the product of mere accident or caprice or, on the other hand, of any deliberate agreement among poets. Their sources are subtle and complex in many cases and certainly cannot be described exhaustively, yet there are certain rather obvious facts which help to account for some of the most important features of modern verse. In the first place, the poet of today simply has far more to write about than did his predecessors. The world of the modern man has expanded in an astonishing fashion during the present century; it is full of institutions and artifacts and ideas which are totally new. Accompanying this, of course, is an even more dramatic increase in man's knowledge and interests. We live today not only with products but with concepts which were undreamt of a generation or so ago. And the poet who writes about the sea or the stars, the city or the human personality, is writing about phenomena which have been redefined radically in our time. Thanks largely to scientists of various sorts, these things have become both immeasurably more complex and, quite possibly, more interesting as objects of both scientific and non-scientific attention.

With the growth of our knowledge has come a change in many of our values. As an example, we have fundamentally, if somewhat gradually, altered our notions of what is "important." In a sense, the world of today contains no trivia. For the data of the natural scientist lie everywhere, while the majority of social scientists derive their greatest insights from the observation of what is commonplace. The effect of this change upon many poets is clearly discernible. It would be very dangerous today to attempt a distinction between subjects which are intrinsically worthy of the poet's attention and those which are not. The modern poet can write seriously and movingly about "little" things, ordinary people, the simple particulars of everyday existence. He has not, one feels, necessarily lost his sense of what is sublime or heroic or profound, but he has gained the capacity to discover these qualities in the ordinary fabric of the world which surrounds him. This disappearance of a doctrine of the inherently "poetic" is reflected not only in the poet's choice of subjects but in his language as well. The notion that a special area of speech can be defined as "poetic diction" has few adherents among today's poets, who are cheerfully prepared to draw upon the language of ordinary conversation, of popular songs, of journalism and advertising, as well as of other lands. For all of these sorts of language *become* "poetic," entirely by virtue of the context of sound and substance in which they are employed.

An age of inquiry and discovery shakes up values in more ways than one. Old orthodoxies, governing not only what is important but what is socially desirable or objectively "real" or "true," tend to be suspended and even abandoned. Often they are replaced by new doctrines, but perhaps as often, in our age, they yield to a certain skepticism: an inquiring, critical frame of mind which is quick to discern the inadequacy of old views but reluctant to substitute dogmatic new ones. This is not to say that the modern poet is without moral conviction or even that he is lacking in traditional religious faith. It is, however, to suggest his unwillingness to abide by Pope's dictum that "whatever is, is right," or to suppress his individual view of things in favor of producing whatever will impress his readers as agreeable. The power, which many poets have always had, to pierce beneath the surfaces of things and to view the phenomena of life in unusual but revealing aspects tends today to be employed in the service of a kind of dispassionate criticism. In many of today's poems, for example, you may sense the poet's unwillingness to submit to pat resolutions or simple, reassuring formulas. For the modern poet is often driven to recognize what is paradoxical and inconsistent: the discrepancy between what men profess to be and what they

133

are, the inextricable blending of good and evil, serious and absurd, extraordinary and commonplace in human experience.

Of all the recent developments in our knowledge and our attitudes, none has more profoundly affected poetry than those concerned with the human personality. The operations of our minds and emotions, the motives for our actions, the nature of our relationships with other people have all been explored and revealed in a new and remarkably complex light. Inevitably, the poet's treatment of the human personality has been affected radically by these discoveries. Human experience can no longer be satisfactorily viewed as a neat series of overt, sequential activities, nor can human character be assessed in any save the most fragmentary way by the use of a traditional vocabulary. The poet who seeks to capture the quality of human thought recognizes that orderly syntactical statement is at most a translation of, a sign for, the processes which are involved in the human consciousness. Thus, in an effort to reach closer to the real quality of human awareness, many poets of our day have abandoned the neat structures, the reasoned propositions, the clear, unequivocal words and syntax of conventional expression. Instead we can expect their poetry often to be organized by the same kinds of forces which govern our thoughts—the involuntary associations and relationships, memories and anticipations, observations and imaginings which defy conventional dimensions of time and space and unconcernedly cross and recross the gap between fact and fancy.

The contemporary influences mentioned thus far are those to which the poet is exposed in essentially the same way as are most modern men—although, of course, we are concerned with his particular response as a poet. We must also recognize the many ways in which the contemporary poet is likely to be affected by the work of other poets—in particular, the work of his immediate and his more remote predecessors. Indeed it is characteristic (although not uniquely so) of modern poets to reveal quite openly a dependence upon their predecessors and to probe, as T. S. Eliot has done, the relationship between "tradition and the individual talent." It is impossible, of course, to establish the precise effect of the poet's predecessors and contemporaries upon the character of any given poem. At the same time, it is possible to indicate certain general problems and areas of concern which more or less regularly have occupied the poets of the recent past and even (although we shall not attempt it here) to note conspicuous innovations by individual poets who have thus provided influences upon their successors.

The climate of this century, on the whole, has been hospitable to experiment, and the experiments of poets have taken many forms. In general, for example, they have shown an interest in exploiting the connotative power of language to a greater degree than ever before. At the sacrifice of unequivocal clarity, many of them have been willing to pursue, to an unprecedented extent, the use of *symbols*. Now symbols are not mere images nor are they simple figurative devices. They are terms which have the power to evoke, through association, images, concepts, and feelings which are, so to speak, greater than the terms themselves. Thus, for example, the flag is the symbol for the nation, not because it resembles the nation but because, largely as a result of historical conditioning, we allow it to waken within us the concept of the nation. In their use of symbols, some modern poets make rather exacting demands upon the reader, requiring that he provide the necessary associations by sharing the knowledge or experience on which the poem draws and even, as in the case of some of Yeats's poetry, that he become familiar with a "private" system of symbols developed by the poet himself.

Modern poetry, moreover, frequently relies in rather novel

ways upon the use of figurative language. We have discovered that the traditional use of similes and metaphors is ordinarily to illuminate one thing by comparison with another. But in certain modern poems, figures are employed in a manner which defies reduction to a simple comparison between two clearly definable things. Often we must make imaginative leaps and summon up associations in order to sense qualities which very different kinds of phenomena have in common. Thus, in T. S. Eliot's "The Love Song of J. Alfred Prufrock," we have the line, "I have measured out my life with coffee spoons." Here the speaker's life is being compared to an un-defined "something," but the important fact is that this some-thing—which really needs no further definition—is capable of being measured out in minute, uniform, genteel doses. If one element in the comparison is vague, the total effect is not. Again, we should remember that the *purpose* of figurative lan-guage in modern poetry may well be something different from the illumination of one thing by comparison with another. When, again in "Prufrock," the speaker describes the time of day "when the evening is spread out against the sky like a pa-tient etherised upon a table," the chief effect is to illuminate neither the evening nor the sky but the condition of the mind to which such a bizarre image suggests itself.

In the use of *images*, without necessary regard to their fig-urative or symbolic value, the modern poet is again often pre-pared to move beyond what can be easily described in logical terms. Influenced, as has been previously suggested, by new views of the human consciousness, the poet is sometimes will-ing to appeal to several senses concurrently, to blend the ab-stract and the concrete, the real and imaginary, the temporal and spatial in an "illogical" but emotionally intelligible amal-gam. And what may appear "strange" in terms of conventional modes of expression achieves, in this way, an unprecedented "reality," to the extent that it approaches the true condition of sensory, emotional, and intellectual experience. Similarly, *ambiguity*, which in much traditional verse as in ordinary communication is generally regarded as a defect, has often been deliberately employed by modern poets on the ground that the very diversity of suggested meanings and associations is a source of poetic richness.

In their concern for making the most effective use of *sounds*, many poets of today and the recent past have rejected the traditional rules of prosody—and, for that matter, some of the rules of syntax, grammar, and vocabulary. There have been poets who have at times attempted to achieve their principal effects through the physical qualities of sound, even at the sacrific of discernible substantive content. Less extravagant efforts have been undertaken by those to whom rhythm and tempo are more important than ordinary syntax. Various poets have attempted to substitute for traditional prosodic systems their own principles of meter: one of the most interesting of these is Gerard Manley Hopkins, who advanced and employed an elaborate theory of "sprung rhythm," on the ground that it most closely approximated the natural rhythms of speech, prose, and music. Beneath these innovations, however, is a reliance on the same fundamental qualities of sound which are exploited in the orderly organization of older verse. Freed from the need to adhere to strict prosodic rules, the modern poet, in fact, often makes strikingly profitable use of rhythm, pitch, and tempo and devotes himself uninhibitedly to experiments in which the sound of words conveys the effect for which he is seeking.

It is clear that many of the innovations we have been discussing make rather special demands upon the reader. Perhaps more than at any other period, the reader of today's verse is asked to exercise his imagination, to draw inferences, provide associations, note differences and similarities. He is often asked as well to share with the poet in rather special kinds of knowledge. Frequently, too, he is required to suspend his traditional views of organization or structure. The "situation," "plot," or "argument" which ordinarily lend order to older poetry are sometimes (although by no means always) difficult to discern in modern poems. On the other hand, the reader will often find a kind of "logic of imagery' of the sort which, as we have discovered, provides the most important structural principle in a poem like Keats's "To Autumn." On occasion the modern poet who seeks to reproduce the order of thoughts as they actually occur in the human mind will exploit a process of association which, while it has little in common with logical reasoning, is natural enough to be entirely intelligible. There are, as well, other novel principles on which the modern poet may choose to organize his work: he may strive, for example, to follow forms suggested by music, dancing, or the visual arts; he may suspend all concern for conventional order in seeking to capture the sounds or movements of natural or artificial phenomena, such as the sea or a locomotive.

We cannot expect to leave all modern poems with the sensation of having pursued a thought to an entirely logical conclusion, resolved with relief a suspense-filled plot, or experienced the kind of emotion which can be easily described. For there are poems which serve as the beginning rather than the end to our reflections, prompt us to our own speculations, or elicit from us uneasy emotional responses which cannot be readily described or readily terminated. Such poems are not necessarily artless or incomplete, for a continuing experience may be precisely what they seek to set in motion, although in this respect they may appear to differ particularly dramatically from traditional poetic theory and practice. For the discoveries of the contemporary world have not made easier but far more difficult the answers to man's basic questions. In its willingness to explore, to question, to scrutinize all data, as well as in its humility and uncertainty in arriving at firm answers, contemporary poetry reflects the intellectual temper of our time.

But although the demands of modern poetry seem to differ from those to which we have become accustomed in older verse, these differences are, for the most part, of degree rather than of kind. We are, at most, asked by the modern poet to "stretch" our abilities to infer, imagine, associate, remember. If Ezra Pound requires that we know or find the meaning of an Italian phrase, Alexander Pope has asked that we remember enough about the *Iliad* to appreciate its derisive echoes in "The Rape of the Lock." If it is mere common sense that we admire, then surely Ben Jonson's "Drink to me only with thine eyes" is a senseless injunction. And if a contemporary poet seems chiefly to rely upon the power of apparently disassociated images, we encounter much the same thing in Coleridge's "Kubla Khan."

There is, then, enough about the representative poetry of our day to permit our setting it apart in certain ways from what has gone before, to challenge us with certain new problems, and to reward us with certain new pleasures. At the same time, the basic elements upon which the poet relies are unchanging, and his demands upon us remain, fundamentally, that we exercise feeling, imagination, and thought. These facts will become more apparent if we consider a fairly representative modern poem together with an equally representative and very well-known traditional work. In examining these two

139

poems, we may discover that some of the "problems" of a modern poem can be found, in some measure, in older works, and that the contemporary poet, whatever novelty we may find in his performance, builds upon a timeless foundation, the unchanging power of language to communicate and to move. Here then is Wordsworth's famous poem, "The Daffodils," written in the early nineteenth century, followed by "Repose of Rivers," the work of Hart Crane, who died tragically in 1932 at the age of thirty-three.

The Daffodils

I wandered lonely as a cloud
That floats on high o'er vales and hills,
When all at once I saw a crowd,
A host, of golden daffodils;
Beside the lake, beneath the trees,
Fluttering and dancing in the breeze.

Continuous as the stars that shine
And twinkle on the milky way,
They stretched in never-ending line
Along the margin of a bay:
Ten thousand saw I at a glance,
Tossing their heads in sprightly dance.

The waves beside them danced; but they
Out-did the sparkling waves in glee.
A poet could not but be gay,
In such a jocund company:
I gazed—and gazed—but little thought
What wealth the show to me had brought:

For oft, when on my couch I lie
In vacant or in pensive mood,
They flash upon that inward eye
Which is the bliss of solitude;
And then my heart with pleasure fills,
And dances with the daffodils.

Repose of Rivers[1]

The willows carried a slow sound,
A sarabande the wind mowed on the mead.
I could never remember
That seething, steady leveling of the marshes
Till age had brought me to the sea.

Flags, weeds. And remembrance of steep alcoves
Where cypresses shared the noon's
Tyranny; they drew me into hades almost.
And mammoth turtles climbing sulphur dreams
Yielded, while sun-silt rippled them
Asunder . . .

How much would I have bartered! the black gorge
And all the singular nestings in the hills
Where beavers learn stitch and tooth.
The pond I entered once and quickly fled—
I remember now its singing willow rim.

And finally, in that memory all things nurse;
After the city that I finally passed
With scalding unguents spread and smoking darts
The monsoon cut across the delta
At gulf gates . . . There beyond the dykes

I heard wind flaking sapphire, like this summer,
And willows could not hold more steady sound.

For all the striking differences between these two poems, the reader will probably note a similarity between the experiences on which they are based. In each a "speaker" has been exposed to phenomena of external nature. In each he has been unable to respond fully at a previous time to what he has seen and felt. And in each the power of the original spectacle is ultimately felt in recollection or memory. Having pointed out this common substantive foundation which the poems share, we may, it appears, have exhausted the points of similarity be-

[1] From *Collected Poems of Hart Crane* by Hart Crane (New York: Liveright Publishing Corp., 1933). By permission of the publishers.

tween the two. Certainly, unless like a library card catalogue we classify poems by "subject matter," we must recognize here that we are dealing with works of different kinds. And yet we must remain sensitive to the fact that in their most basic procedures and in the most basic demands they make upon the reader, Wordsworth and Crane present important points of resemblance.

Particularly when compared to Crane's verse, "The Daffodils" may strike us as an unusually direct, unambiguous, and simple account of an experience the speaker has had. But throughout the poem we are actually required to suspend our notions of what is "literally true," to grasp and respond to relatively strange comparisons, and ultimately to accept an experience which has elements both of ambiguity and mystery. In short, a rather plausible encounter and a subsequent recollection of it are transformed into a unique vision, intelligible enough if we allow our imaginations to range beside that of the poet, but clearly at variance with the common-sense version of the situation which would be presented if we were concerned only with the "objective" facts.

Even the opening lines of the poem, now so familiar to many of us that we find little that is strange in them, present a simile which is by no means common or unequivocal. To point to the fleeciness, whiteness, or airiness of a cloud for purposes of comparison seems reasonable enough, but we do not ordinarily think of clouds as lonely. The figure, indeed, may place some strain upon our customary view of clouds. Yet what the simile lacks in concreteness is more than made up by the diversity of its implications. As the figure is developed, the wanderer appears not only "solitary" (in the sense that a single cloud appears isolated from its fellows), but also as somewhat remote from the earth, over which he proceeds with a kind of cloud-like, random mobility.

We sense how dramatic is the spectacle of the daffodils because it has the power to arrest the detached aimless wanderer. But in the description of the flowers, Wordsworth is again by no means conventional. The color of the daffodils—ordinarily a quality which might receive the greatest attention in a description of flowers—is mentioned only once. Instead, the emphasis is upon quantity and motion. To achieve this, the poet employs a tacit comparison with a huge number of dancing people—or at least animate creatures of some sort. What has been conveyed here is a highly personalized *impression*—an impression which, conditioned by the speaker's previous solitude and aimlessness, is of a crowd engaged in more or less concerted activity. To convey this impression, the poet has suppressed the mention of many things which we might expect from a more balanced or objective account of the spectacle and, at the same time, has stressed those aspects of the sight which serve to enforce and unify the impression itself. Thus the water beside which the flowers grow is used not, as might be expected, for *contrast* in color or texture, but initially to suggest the vast deployment of the mass of daffodils and subsequently as an object of *comparison*, sharing in inferior degree the dancing liveliness of the flowers.

The "human" aspect of the daffodils is regularly developed. The initial terms "crowd" and "host" are traditionally applicable to people; in the second stanza, the flowers actually "toss their heads in sprightly dance." It is not surprising, therefore, that in the third stanza both flowers and waves are assigned the human emotion of glee or that the poet's response to the spectacle reveals that his loneliness has been replaced by a sensation expressed in terms ordinarily used to describe genuine human fellowship.

What is most extraordinary about the total experience has yet to occur and is, as the concluding couplet of the third

143

stanza indicates, undreamt of by the speaker himself at the time of his actual exposure to the flowers. For the closest union between the daffodils and the poet occurs when the latter —again solitary, but immobile now and temporally and spatially remote from the flowers—feels the heart within him join the daffodils in their dance.

This "miracle" is attributable in part to the power of the flowers but also to the "inward eye," which is accordingly a crucial element in the climactic final stanza of the poem. The inward eye is an image of a rather vague sort, but it is more than that. It serves to suggest to us both the imagination and the memory, a capacity which cannot be defined or actually attributed to any organ of the body yet which is responsible for recapturing and intensifying past experience so as to serve as "the bliss of solitude." Though it would be difficult to assign a satisfactory denotative meaning to the term, its connotations are rich and—for the purposes of the poem—satisfactory. There is nothing to prevent our equating the "inward eye" with some particular faculty or, on the other hand, allowing it to remain vaguely suggestive of man's general gift for finding solace in memory and imagination. And thus the term is a symbol—a phrase which, taken literally, may seem thin or bewildering or illogical, but which is capable of eliciting from us, in this context, associations that are meaningful and satisfying.

In its more formal aspects, "The Daffodils" will probably strike the reader as a thoroughly "traditional" poem; its syntax is conventional and logical, and its uniform tetrameter lines, with a strongly prevailing iambic rhythm, are (despite ingenious variations) rather strikingly regular. But this very regularity is not the product of servile deference to rules but rather of the poet's deliberate choice. In the poem there are many elements—prosody, syntax, language, and the sequential narrative order—which are deliberately simple. Yet the simplicity of these things should not mislead us as to the character of the poem as a whole. Rather the simplicity serves to contrast with and to make more eloquent an experience which is not only unusual and, in a sense, "magical," but which supplies us as well with an extraordinary view concerning the power of nature to affect the sensibilities of man.

On a first reading, "Repose of Rivers" may appear to offer considerable challenge to our understanding. We may be puzzled by the sentence structure or lack thereof, by the curious juxtaposition of familiar words, by the absence of an apparent sequence of events or even of thoughts. And yet the moderately sensitive and honest reader should find that his first experience with the poem produces, at the least, a certain mood —the impression of a nostalgic, belatedly achieved memory, of images which, though diversified, possess coherence and awaken genuine sensations. If we do feel such a mood, the poem has already achieved a major effect, for there is, quite plainly, no exposition of logical propositions, no hidden allegorical "meaning" to be ferreted out from a work of this sort. On the other hand, as inquiring students of poetry, we should be interested in the actual poetic sources of the impressions we have gained and hopeful, as well, that a recognition of those sources will augment and clarify the impressions themselves.

The fact that the poem may be regarded as the representation—and, implicitly, the attempted re-creation—of a mood should help to explain the apparent quality of disorder which may strike some readers. For, as we have earlier suggested, the poet of today is likely to be concerned with the actual quality of human feelings and reflections rather than with their translation into orderly and entirely intelligible language. If,

145

therefore, the images of this poem seem fragmentary and incapable of unification into a single, consistent sensory experience, if sentences seem incomplete or oddly arranged, if temporal sequence seems garbled, we should recognize in these phenomena something of the quality with which, in truth, the imagination contemplates past experience. At the same time, it is improper and unjust to say that the poetic structure proceeds along no other principle than the random operations of human fancy. For, as we shall try to suggest, the effect created by this poem is the product of an artistic care which is fully as deliberate as, if less obvious than, that which we found in "The Daffodils."

In this work, as in many other modern poems, the title can be regarded not only as a helpful preliminary "clue," but as virtually a part of the poem itself. Here indeed it is a uniquely explicit statement (for neither "repose" nor "rivers" are again mentioned literally) about the kind of natural phenomenon and the kind of abstract quality which are the objects of the poet's attention. But the actual poetic procedure by which this "topic" is developed and illuminated appears to be a sort of "plot," the order of events which is summarized by the words "I could never remember . . . till age had brought me to the sea." What it is that the speaker could not remember and the circumstances which finally produce the memory are, quantitatively at least, the major preoccupation of the poet, but it is the sequential action, the memory lost and recovered, which furnishes the "excuse" for the poem.

Implicit in this plot-like principle of structure there is also "character" of a sort, and it is here that we encounter one of the most interesting problems presented by the poem. The recovery of memory is plainly an experience which is undergone by the speaker, the "I" of the poem. And, to judge by what we have seen in other poetic works, our response to what happens in the poem may be largely determined by our view of the identity—of the moral and intellectual qualities—of this speaker.

But who is the speaker? We can imagine this question being answered by a thoughtful reader (let us call him Mr. Smith) somewhat as follows:

"The speaker of the poem is simply an anonymous 'I,' about whom—like the speaker, say, in 'Delight in Disorder'—we do not need to infer anything more than what is made quite clear in the poem itself. He is a person, perhaps a poet, who is sensitive and nostalgic. Now, at the time of writing, he is older than he was when he underwent the experience which is the genesis of the poem. He has wandered and searched, moving systematically or otherwise down the length of a river, and he has eventually recovered his original experience. Beyond these facts, all questions about his character and identity are entirely irrelevant."

But here a second, equally thoughtful reader (conveniently if unimaginatively named Mr. Jones) offers a very different opinion. Here is the argument he puts forward:

"The words in 'Repose of Rivers' are not those of a person at all. They are clearly spoken by the river itself! Even the title suggests this, for it speaks of the repose *of* rivers, an experience which rivers themselves undergo. What beside a river is 'drawn' into steep alcoves, 'enters' and 'flees' the pond, and 'passes' the city? It is a river, and only a river, which, inevitably, 'age' brings 'to the sea.' Moreover, the episodes which are experienced do not involve descriptions of the river itself, as it would be observed by a person, but of its surroundings and inhabitants—the kinds of things the river would 'notice' as it moves from the marshy meadows, through varied kinds of scenery, to ultimate union with the ocean."

We can imagine the dialogue continuing, perhaps rather heatedly:

"Your interpretation," Smith might say, "is typically 'fancy' and unnecessary. If the repose is *of* the river, can't it be observed and shared by a human being? Of course rivers may be said to enter and leave, to be drawn into places, or to pass through them. But cannot humans as well? What's more, are rivers sentient, able to hear sounds? Do they remember, or try to remember? Can you imagine a wilder image than that of a river which is desperately anxious to barter something in exchange for a lost memory? What possible use is it to impose such an extravagant interpretation on a poem which, as it stands, allows us to see its central action as a perfectly intelligible and moving *human* quest?"

"My dear fellow," Jones puts in, "you seem to forget that this is a *poem*. You are insisting that the poet confine himself to mere physical fact and that whatever is 'intelligible,' as you put it, conform precisely to literal experience. To me, the charm of the poem is enormously enhanced by the delightful notion that a river moves because it is in search of something which it knew only at its origin. Personification of this kind is certainly a respectable poetic device. And here it has been used to suggest something that is quite lovely and certainly not disturbingly strange—namely, that a river has a soul and a changing life of its own, that it is a questing, often troubled, creature which recovers its original repose only when it joins the sea."

"You seem intent," Smith rejoins, "on reducing the poem to a level which is childish and banal. Pleasant enough poems have purported to be the 'songs' which rivers sing,[2] but if you insist on turning this poem into such an affair, you will be robbing it of much of its real interest. For I insist that human memories, human searches, wanderings, frustrations, and triumphs are basically more interesting than whatever feelings and adventures we may fancifully attribute to a river. And it certainly seems silly to 'read into' the poem an interpretation which is less engaging than the most obvious and sensible meaning which the words provide."

At this point it seems likely that Jones sputters violently, protesting that it is the function of poetry to get away from what is "obvious and sensible" and into the realm of what is subtle and imaginative. Smith in turn may snort and mutter that there is certainly a distinction between productive imagination and totally unwarranted fantasy. We ourselves—eavesdroppers at the controversy—may feel that our attempts to understand the nature of lyric poetry have received a severe setback.

For it is obvious that a discussion of this sort does not resolve the problem of the speaker's identity and, indeed, may create some uneasiness over the idea that two such very different notions may follow from careful readings of a single work. Yet whether we accept one or the other opinion, advance our own (entirely different) hypothesis, or suspend final judgment as to the identity of the speaker, our fundamental understanding of the poem and our pleasure in reading it are not really affected. For here we are in the presence of precisely the sort of *ambiguity* which, whether deliberate or not, sets us to thinking, remembering, and associating—which,

[2] Smith doubtless has in mind such favorites as Tennyson's "The Brook" or Sidney Lanier's "The Song of the Chattahoochee," both of which the conscientious reader can find in many anthologies.

that is, initiates within us those activities of the reason and imagination which are the mark of authentic participation in the poetic experience. As our imaginary dialogue suggests, the answers which two different readers offer to such a question as the identity of a "speaker" may legitimately vary and may shape, in some measure, their separate responses to the poem. But the two views of the work are not basically incompatible, nor do they determine which reader will receive the greater satisfaction from the work. Moreover, both views follow directly and demonstrably from what can be read in the poem, from particular assertions and their relationship in an integrated work of art. These interpretations are not, that is, the product of whimsical or accidental association, nor is the poem here treated—as poems sometimes are—as a springboard to be neglected as soon as it catapults the reader into his private world of recollection and revery.

The ambiguity of this poem is the ambiguity which lends force to the meaning of the word *lyric*. Whatever structural support is afforded by plot, whatever consistency may be found in character, and whatever appeals are made to our own natural interest in certain aspects of "actuality," are, in such a poem as "Repose of Rivers," subordinate to the effect achieved by the imagery and music of language. In this instance, that is, the power of the poet's words asserts itself independently, and whether we view the words as those of a poet or of a river remains a secondary question. Indeed, the ambiguous identity of the speaker may be regarded as an additional source of richness, for it invites us to augment the effects of image and sound with those associations which, while authentically invited by the poem, appear most reasonable and congenial.

To speak of the creation of *mood* is, in this instance, far from idle. The poem proceeds by a series of evocative images.

Their primary function is neither to advance plot nor to illuminate character, but this does not mean that they are not related systematically. It only means that, in an analytical account of the poem, we should concentrate upon sound and image and upon the feelings they elicit.

Each of the four long stanzas, then, can be seen as a group of images which are, in effect, the objects of memory. These groups have in common an association with the river, although, since these associations vary greatly in the degree of their proximity to the river, we might very well neglect this common bond if it were not for the title of the poem. Each group of images, moreover, seems to possess a unity of its own, achieved by concentration on a relatively unified aspect of the river (or a river) and a single, if rather general, sensation which the aspect thus chosen produces.

Thus in the initial stanza we have, in addition to the statement of the "plot" itself, a group of images which appeal to the senses of sound and sight as well as to a combination of both (as in the image of the willows "carrying sound" or the sarabande, which, being a dance, carries inevitable suggestions of music). The river here is willow-lined and its surroundings are level and regular; the sounds and movements which accompany the spectacle are similarly regular and undisturbed. This is the river in "repose," but of a particular kind, based not upon silence or somnolence, but upon sounds, movements, and contours which are uninterrupted and unchanging.

A very different aspect of the river (or conceivably a different river) appears in the second stanza. Whatever repose we find here is a fitful half-sleep, engendered yet threatened by the fierce heat of a summer noon. The literal imagery is clear enough: marsh plants, dark cypresses, and the sluggish turtles, restlessly stirring in patches of broken sunlight. To the "speaker" who beholds the scene, however, the "steep alcoves'" seem as a descent into hell, where huge creatures stir uneasily in "sulphur dreams" beneath the sun's rays (themselves fragmented and scattered like the silt upon the river bed). This is the river, sunlit and sinister beneath a heat which can subdue and destroy.

A reminder of the "plot," the problem of gaining lost memory, begins the third stanza. We find it in the fragmentary exclamation, "How much I would have bartered"—apparently an expression of frustrated longing to recover the recollection of repose. Here the river is seen as a gorge among the hills, a secret thing, surrounded by the hidden nests of birds, the quiet working of beavers. There is song here and, like the sounds of the first stanza, it is heard among the willows; but in this instance it is abruptly encountered, briefly heard, hastily fled from. The river and its surroundings possess a privacy not to be invaded save accidentally and briefly; if there is repose in this aspect of the river it is not to be shared by the intruder.

The fourth stanza leads to the brink of recovery, but not before the speaker has encountered the pain and terror of the city which lies at the delta of the river—the ultimate, savage antithesis of the repose whose memory he is seeking, yet a part too of the total memory in which "all things nurse."[3] The noon heat has become a scalding oil, an unguent which, perversely, brings pain instead of relief; the sun's rays have become fierce darts in the city smoke; the musical wind is now

[3] The statement, ". . . in that memory all things nurse," seems to provide the most satisfactory meaning if we consider "nurse" as an intransitive verb: the words can then be paraphrased to some such effect as "in that memory all things take nourishment." At the same time, the very ambiguity of the verb invites a very different interpretation of the phrase as meaning that something occurs "in that memory (which) all things nurse" and, although this reading is difficult to justify in this particular syntactical context, there is no reason why it should not provide "overtones" which are concurrent with the more "logical" interpretation.

the destructive monsoon. But beyond the city at the river's mouth is the sea, and it is here, as we have been told in the first stanza, that memory is recovered and that repose is gained.

Though one finds in the concluding two lines another "illogical" blend of sensory images, the final description of the sea is clear in its effect. For the speaker finds in the sound of the wind, as it "flakes" the sapphire-blue sea in waves, the memory which has been lost—the sense of steadiness and repose which the first stanza has described.

The poem, then, can be seen very simply as one which tells of the repose found in an initial experience, of a pursuit of the memory of that experience through a number of other experiences, and of the recovery of that memory through a final, similar experience, this time by the sea. Even this simple account is sufficient to impose a satisfactory principle of order upon the rich collections of images which are more memorable in themselves than is the "plot" which brings them into being.

But in a thorough reading of the poem we recognize that the poet is concerned with the rather complex operations of memory as well as with things remembered, and this recognition imposes on the work a series of temporal levels which, while they may complicate our reading, bring the poem closer to the realities of human imagination. From such phrases as "till age had brought me to the sea" and "like this summer," we infer that the poet is speaking in a "present" which is temporally separated from the whole process of search and discovery he is describing. Thus the poem is the "memory" of how a memory was recaptured. Moreover, each stage in the "search" for the original, reposeful memory of the river—through the sleepy, sun-lit hades, the secret black gorge, and the terror of the city—becomes a memory itself, or at least part of a single great memory in which "all things nurse." Beyond this, it is apparent that "memory" and "remembering" are used in the poem in ways which, though they may defy clinical definition, assume a function which is close to that of a symbol. For it is clear that memory here is not the mere recollection of incident or spectacle or even sound alone, but rather the recovery, the re-experiencing of a unique moment of sensory and emotional awareness—to be described, as it is here, in terms of an intangible impression of reposeful steadiness, produced by a special response to sound and movement, color and texture.

Seen in this light, the poem offers a rather subtle but not particularly "strange" account of a phenomenon which most readers can readily imagine and with which, indeed, many of them may be very familiar. It may, in fact, be argued that the substance of "Repose of Rivers" coincides far more closely with the data of human experience than does the mystical response to natural beauty reported in "The Daffodils." The reader may, however, still feel that there is, in Crane's poem, a rather unnecessary singularity in prosody and syntax; yet a brief examination into this question should reveal that here again the poet has made choices which are entirely reasonable in terms of the effect which he is seeking.

While the metrical characteristics of the poem are not sufficiently uniform to allow our imposing on it a traditional classification, we should be aware of rhythms which occur often enough to establish a prevailing pattern, departures from which are conspicuous—and are made precisely for that reason. Of the poem's twenty-three lines, in fact, thirteen are essentially in iambic pentameter and, although some of them present slight but eloquent variations (through the use of a feminine ending or the introduction of an extra internal syllable), at least four, including the final line of the poem, are completely regular.

We can discover how the pattern is established and also sense the effect achieved by departure from it by examining the first three lines of the poem. Thus the first line is a tetrameter in which two regular iambs are followed by a pyrrhic and a spondee. The second line is pentameter, with only a substitute trochee in the fourth foot to vary its iambic beat. The third line, however, is dramatically different from the two which precede it; it can be described as two trochees, followed by an iamb, to which an extra syllable has been added to produce a feminine ending. Breaking in as it does upon the serene account of satisfying sensory experience, this contrasting tetrameter, with its harsh prose rhythms, stridently announces that the reposeful images which have preceded are, in fact, the object of the speaker's frustrated search.

A similarly "functional" account may be given for much of the irregularity in the rest of the poem. To take one rather obvious example, we note that the word "asunder" constitutes the whole of a single line at the end of the second stanza. The effect it achieves in this position is clear, for having been lulled into a kind of false repose by the image and the rhythms of "sun-silt rippled them," we are made abruptly aware that, for the speaker, the fragments of sunlight appear strangely destructive. Here, as in the word "tyranny" in the third line of the stanza, we have what may appear to be a prosodic eccentricity—a gratuitous "run-on" which seems particularly unnecessary in view of the latitude of line length the poet enjoys. But actually the poet has exploited this latitude by employing the new line as a device which entertainers, among others, have made familiar; he has, that is, introduced "at the last moment" a word which completely upsets our expectation and radically alters the apparent meaning of what has gone before.

Despite the absence of end rhymes in the poem, Crane has made as abundant use of repetition as we are likely to find in any rhymed verse. It hardly seems necessary to point out, even in the first stanza, the frequency with which alliteration, assonance, and consonance appear—the identity, for example, of all save the vowel sound in "mowed" and "mead," or the way in which "seething, steady, leveling" is a sort of continuous chain in which the first and last terms are linked to the central word by alliteration and assonance respectively. The word "sarabande," remarkable enough for the image it creates, makes a strong appeal to the ear alone. Its initial and final consonants have already appeared in the same position in the word "sound" (and both are repeated strikingly at other points in the stanza). But in "sarabande" these sounds now mark the beginning and end of a three-syllable word, whose first and last syllables produce an agreeable "internal" assonance of their own. This is not mere repetition; it is repetition with variation, employed as in music, for purposes of genuine development—of a progression in sound which, in its growing complexity and richness, matches the parallel progression of imagery.

Within the total context of the poem, repetition is obviously employed to achieve unity, as we can see by comparing the final two lines with the whole of the first stanza. Here, substantively, the cycle has been completed and the initial experience of the river has been recaptured by the experience with the sea. To match this substantive resolution, we find not only the literal repetition of words (in addition to "sound," which ends the last line as it did the first, five other terms are repeated), but the initial *s* and terminal *d*, crucially important in the first stanza, variously recurrent throughout the poem, and here powerfully repeated to enforce the unifying character of the final experience.

From what has been said of substance, language, and sound, the student should by now recognize that beneath the apparently casual quality of this poem lie a number of firm structural principles which provide both unity and variety to the work. Many other evidences of artful organization could be pointed out. We might note, for example, the curious reappearance of the notion of "inability," professed by the speaker in the "I could never remember" of the first stanza but transformed into an affirmation in the final line: "And willows could not hold more steady sound." Again we might be aware of several "themes" in the imagery which recur in shifting contexts and with widely varied effects. One such might be called the theme of "destruction" or "attack." It is first apparent in the benign "mowing" of the wind, reappears in the sinister destructiveness of the sun, is suggested by the "stitch and tooth" of the beavers, emerges in its most terrible aspect in the "scalding unguents," "smoking darts," and (fierce echo of its earlier mowing) the monsoon which cuts across the delta. Seen as the final, resolving stage in this succession, the phrase "flaking sapphire" loses none of its strange beauty but gains a special appropriateness by its appeal to the "logic of imagery."

The examination of particular features in Crane's poem has not been calculated to alter in any major way our original response to the work. The response remains primarily one of "mood"—of feeling something of the satisfaction and wonder which accompany the recovery of an elusive experience, of the quality of the experience itself, as well as of its pursuit and ultimate recapture. We have attempted to suggest, however, that the mood is the product of a poetic procedure which—despite its appearance as a random, "natural" reflection of images and impressions—actually involves a systematic development within a firmly unified structure. If we cannot precisely define the feelings which the poem elicits from us, we can at least recognize that they result, in part at least, from our ability to share with the poet in his sensuous and emotional response to certain kinds of spectacle, in the agreeable tension of search, and in the joy of rediscovery and resolution.

Many of the differences we have noted between "The Daffodils" and "Repose of Rivers" must be attributed assuredly to the peculiar poetic individuality of each writer—to the obvious fact that the creation of any poem is a unique occasion. At the same time, there are qualities in each poem which can be traced to influences which shaped the preoccupations and choices of the writer—qualities which an awareness of the poet's *historic* identity may lead us to expect and accept. Thus, for instance, in "The Daffodils," the simplicity of diction, the transparent regularity of meter, and the experience which provides the substance of the poem all exemplify certain beliefs which were carefully developed by Wordsworth and a number of his "Romantic" contemporaries. Knowledge of these beliefs will allow us to find in the "inward eye," for example, far more than a unique, rather cryptic if poetically satisfying, symbolic device. For those who are generally familiar with Wordsworth's thought, the figure will illuminate and receive illumination from such statements by the poet as this one:

I have said that poetry is the spontaneous overflow of powerful feelings: it takes its origin from emotion recollected in tranquillity: the emotion is contemplated till, by a species of reaction, the tranquillity gradually disappears, and an emotion kindred to that which was before the subject of contemplation, is gradually produced and does itself actually exist in the mind.[4]

[4] From the Preface to the second edition of *Lyrical Ballads* (1800).

A poem like "The Daffodils" loses none of its individuality but gains a new dimension of achievement when it is seen as one of many attempts to assert and embody aesthetic beliefs which were widely and deeply held at the time of its composition.

The representative poetry of our own time, strictly speaking, does not require a process of historical recovery in order to be understood and admired. But many of its distinctive qualities—and hence what the common reader is likely to regard as its "problems"—have their source in the poet's historic identity. In effect, the same fundamental kinds of influence, tradition, and preoccupation should be taken into account in reading the poetry of any period. To speak of a poem as "modern" or "Romantic" or "Augustan" is to suggest that its ultimate character is, in some measure, the product of specific historic circumstances.

The chief source of the distinctive character of modern verse lies in a new conception of reality—an awareness that human experience eludes attempts at neat, literal description and can be poetically captured, if at all, when the poet and reader are conscious of its complex, often ambiguous dimensions. This is probably the basis for the common view that modern poety is "difficult." Certainly good modern verse does not invite flabby surrender to the charms of conventional prettiness or banal sentiments. The rivers of the modern poet are not those of the picture post card, nor do his memories echo the simple-minded nostalgia of the popular song. The appreciation of modern poetry requires a kind of worldliness, affirmed by the reader's willingness to direct upon a single poem, if need be, the sum of his experience, his learning, and his powers of inference and imagination. What is not required, however, is "special" knowledge or initiation into a world which lies beyond the experience of the ordinary man. For as men, modern poets are our contemporaries; as poets, they are our spokesmen. At its best, modern verse does not challenge our ingenuity or erudition, but our modernity. Its special characteristics are largely the product of our own age and world. And at its heart is the ageless power of all poetry—the appeal to the eternal human gifts of sympathy, wisdom, and imagination.

INDEX

Imagery, 43, 44, 136, 137
Incident in narration, 75
Issue in narration, 64

Jonson, Ben, 139
Joyce, James, 72

Keats, John, "To Autumn," 42–57

Lines as units of verse, 14–16
Literature, problem of definition, 1–4
Lyric, meaning of term, 4

Masculine ending, 22
Messenger speech, 114
Metaphor, 11
Meter, 17–26
Milton, John, *Paradise Lost*, 90
Modern, as term applied to literature, 131
Monometer, 20
Mood, 56

Narration, dramatic, 114
Narrative poetry, 89–91
Novel, 62

Octave, 28
Omniscient narrator, 71, 72
O'Neill, Eugene, 121
Onomatopoeia, 46, 47
Ottava-rima, 27

Pentameter, 20, 21
Performance, dramatic, 123
Personification, 36
Plot: presence in poetry, 7, 8; in narrative fiction, 63–79; in drama, 108–13
Poetry, problem of definition, 1–3
Point-of-view, 70
Pope, Alexander, 47, 133, 139
Pound, Ezra, 139
Prologue, 105
Proscenium, 118
Prosody, use of term, 29
Pyrrhus, 20

Quatrain, 27

Recognition as element in plot, 76
Repetition as prosodic element, 47–50
Resolution of plot, 64
Reversal as element in plot, 67
Rhyme, 1; as source of structure, 15–17; "strained," 40, 41; internal, 46, 47
Rhythm, 18 n.
Rime royal, 27
Romanticism, 128
Run-on lines, 25

Scenes, dramatic, 119–21
Sestet, 28
Setting: in fiction, 86–88; theatrical, 116
Shakespeare, William: *Romeo and Juliet*, 97–108, 114–17, 122; *Hamlet*, 111, 124, 126; *Othello*, 111, 116
Shaw, George Bernard, 105
Simile, 11
Slack syllables, 17, 18
Soliloquy in drama, 115
Sonnet, 28; definition of types, 28
Sophocles, *Oedipus the King*, 111
Sound: as poetic element, 14, 46–52; in modern verse, 137
Spenserian stanza, 27
Spondee, 19, 20
Sprung rhythm, 137
Stanza, 15, 27
Stevenson, Robert Louis, *Treasure Island*, 60–91
Stressed syllables, 17, 18
Substance of literary work, 6
Substitute foot, 25
Symbols, 12, 135

Tempo, 49–51
Tercet, 27
Terza-rima, 27
Tetrameter, 20
Theater-in-the-round, 118
Theme in fiction, 91, 92